EXCAVATING THE LOST COLONY MYSTERY

EXCAVATING THE LOST COLONY MYSTERY

The Map, the Search, the Discovery

Edited by Eric Klingelhofer

The University of North Carolina Press

Chapel Hill

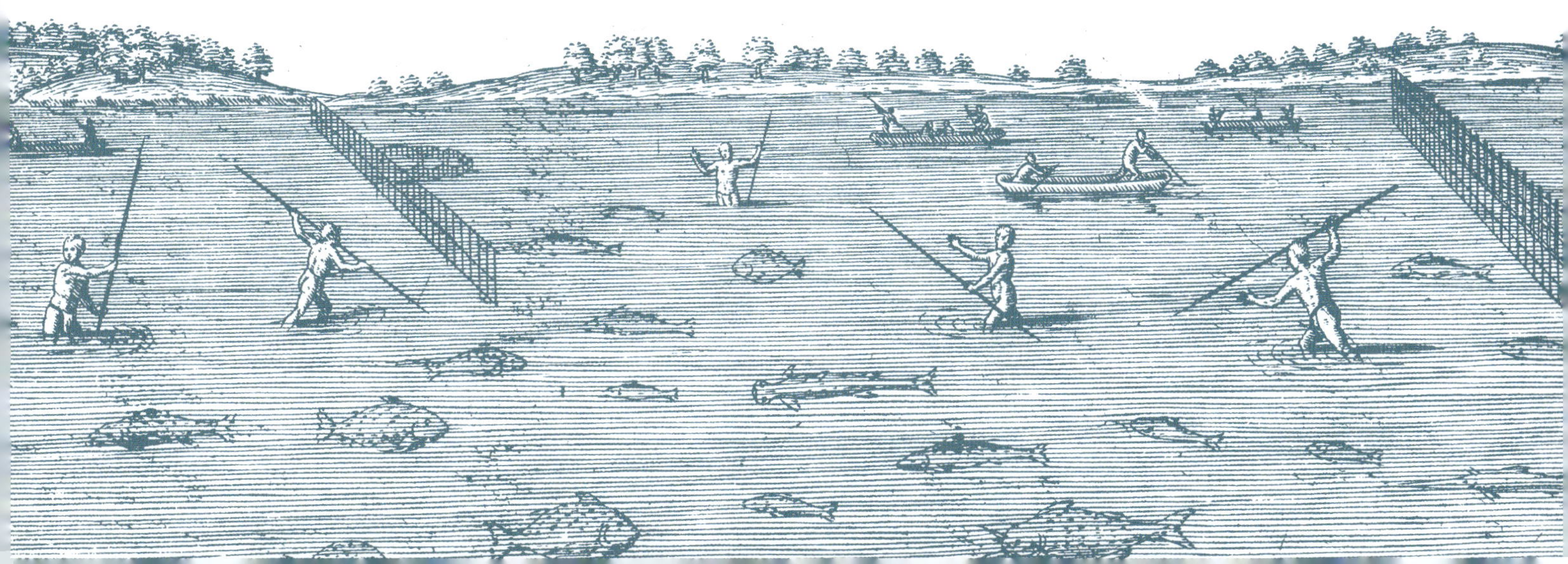

This book was published with the assistance of the Blythe Family Fund of the University of North Carolina Press and supported in part by the British Museum Scholarly Publications Fund, First Colony Foundation, and an anonymous donor.

Designed by Jamison Cockerham
Set in Arno, Scala Sans, Fell DW Pica, and Irby
By Jamie McKee, MacKey Composition

Cover art: *Map of La Virginea Pars*, ca. 1585.
© The Trustees of the British Museum.

Frontispiece: Kim Sloan (*right*) and Janet Ambers show Eric Klingelhofer (*left*) John White's watercolors in the British Museum's Department of Prints and Drawings, 2013. Courtesy of the staff of the Department of Prints and Drawings.

Manufactured in the United States of America

LIBRARY OF CONGRESS
CATALOGING-IN-PUBLICATION DATA
Names: Klingelhöfer, Eric C., editor. | First Colony Foundation (Durham, N.C.), sponsoring body.
Title: Excavating the Lost Colony mystery : the map, the search, the discovery / edited by Eric Klingelhofer.
Other titles: Map, the search, the discovery
Description: Chapel Hill : The University of North Carolina Press, [2023] | Includes bibliographical references and index.
Identifiers: LCCN 2023017144 | ISBN 9781469673752 (cloth ; alk. paper) | ISBN 9781469673769 (ebook)
Subjects: LCSH: Colonists—North Carolina—Roanoke Island—History—16th century. | Excavations (Archaeology)—North Carolina—Fort Raleigh. | Excavations (Archaeology)—North Carolina—Bertie County. | Roanoke Colony. | Roanoke Island (N.C.)—History—16th century. | BISAC: HISTORY / United States / State & Local / South (AL, AR, FL, GA, KY, LA, MS, NC, SC, TN, VA, WV) | HISTORY / Social History
Classification: LCC F229 .E94 2023 | DDC 975.6/17501—dc23/eng/20230425
LC record available at https://lccn.loc.gov/2023017144

In honor of those who blazed the trail

JEAN C. HARRINGTON

DAVID BEERS QUINN

IVOR NOËL HUME

In memory of

JANET AMBERS

Who sought the hidden history
in John White's maps

Contents

Preface

We did not intend to search for the Lost Colony. We had formed First Colony Foundation (FCF) to carry on fieldwork on Roanoke Island, where little progress had been made since its last major archaeological excavation ended in 1992. I was concerned about rapid development of land on Roanoke Island and the simultaneous threat of coastal erosion, and so I contacted my colleagues from the 1990–92 dig at Fort Raleigh National Historic Site. From that experience, we had learned that all traces of Sir Walter Raleigh's colony were very slight and could be recognized only by experts. A unique treasure in American history, they represented the first English colony, a score of years before Jamestown and two score before Plymouth. My colleagues from that project had gone separate ways. Some were leading Jamestown Rediscovery, now Historic Jamestowne, where a flood of artifacts and architectural discoveries excited the public with a new vision of life in that first permanent English colony. The National Park Service ranger historian at Fort Raleigh became a lawyer. I had spent the decade investigating Raleigh's settlements in Ireland and then searching for his traces in the Caribbean.

It was time, we agreed, to pool our skills, energy, and what available time each could spare. But it would not be another one-off dig. Those efforts had produced some results, but after a century of searching, there was still no sign of the fort and settlement that the documents described, and what had been unearthed was not well understood. Nor was there a coherent plan to conduct a systematic search since that of J. C. Harrington in the late 1940s. We prepared to commit ourselves to a long-term research project on all aspects of the Roanoke colonies, their history and archaeology. We took the name of First Colony Foundation, an ambitious name for what we really were, a plucky band of pro-bono professionals without funds. We were soon chartered and chose our lawyer-historian to serve as president to keep us from going astray. Next, we arranged a formal research agreement with the National Park Service and turned our attention to Fort Raleigh. As Phil Evans relates in our first chapter, we were immediately concerned with the eroding shoreline and so tested areas that the park service had not explored. Then we addressed questions raised by the 1990–92 project on the area surrounding the reconstructed earthwork. At the same time, we began the task of finding out what lay beneath the largely unexplored forested sand dunes covering many acres west of the reconstructed earthwork.

First Colony Foundation was created to carry out all forms of research on Raleigh's colonies. That broad program maintained multiple lines of inquiry, which led to much new information about the First Colony of 1585 and later to an important clue to the fate of the Lost Colony of 1587. With unique skills and professional experience, the FCF investigators followed that lead to unearth hard evidence for the fate of at least some of those settler families. Our second chapter tells the story of the hidden symbol in John White's *Virginea Pars* map and how additional information can be found in earlier Tudor maps and in the picture-maps that White drew for Raleigh. Kim Sloan, Peter Barber, and I report on our respective areas of research.

The third chapter covers the archaeological search, as we sought to discover what—if any—evidence there was for Elizabethans in the area indicated by the hidden symbol on the map. Here, I describe the various scientific techniques of remote sensing that we used in the search, Nick Luccketti relates the excavations at Site X, and Clay Swindell describes the Carolina Algonquians who lived in the adjacent village of Mettaquem. The contributions in the next chapter provide valuable context to our discoveries: Karen Kupperman on the great degree in which Elizabethan explorers were informed by—and indebted to—their Indian allies, and Bly Straube on the items that Raleigh's colonists would have brought with them. In the final chapter, Jim Horn explains why the Lost Colonists went west from Roanoke, and Phil Evans looks ahead to the seventeenth century with a history of the later English visitors and settlers in the upper Albemarle Sound.

These contributions are firsthand accounts by the men and women who made the discoveries—in map rooms, in archives, and in the field. It may appear to be a straightforward process of inquiry, but it was no easy task. It was long, hard work, with little compensation other than the pride of having completed another step in the research design, however little most steps actually produced. We succeeded because we took advantage of techniques unavailable to past generations and because we had had spent decades acquiring expertise in our own specific fields of study. And I believe that our reluctance to seek premature publicity gave other professionals confidence in our rigorous scholarship, which has led to a generous and ongoing sharing of information. This book is the result.

Acknowledgments

First Colony Foundation research was initiated with the encouragement of deceased board members William Friday, David Stick, and Ivor Noël Hume. Assistance on this project was provided in North Carolina by the Office of State Archaeology, the University of North Carolina Archaeology Laboratory; in Virginia by Jamestown Rediscovery, now Historic Jamestowne, and the Thomas Jefferson National Accelerator Facility; and overseas by the British Museum, British Library, and Museum of London. The 2017 First Colony Foundation Symposium was funded in part by the Dare County Visitors Bureau, Outer Banks Community Foundation, Meekins Trust, Walter A. Bloedorn Foundation, and a family that has generously supported the Foundation.

Exploration for Site X was funded by a National Geographic–Waitt grant; fieldwork there was made possible by support and assistance from the landowner Michael Flannelly, the Reverend Joseph Cooper, Mrs. Clara Bell, Windsor Mayor Jim Hoggard, John Whitehurst, and local volunteers, especially Madison Phillips and David McCall. In Site Y, the fieldwork and postexcavation analysis was made possible by assistance from the Bertie County Commission and the Town of Windsor. Both projects received grants from the Walter A. Bloedorn Foundation, as well as donations from First Colony Foundation's loyal and generous supporters. As the result of preservation efforts by North Carolina's Coastal Land Trust, both Site X and Mettaquem are now part of the Salmon Creek State Natural Recreation Area. Site Y, though threatened by erosion, lies on Bertie County land dedicated for public recreation. All three sites are preserved as part of North Carolina's heritage.

part one

SEEKING THE TRUTH

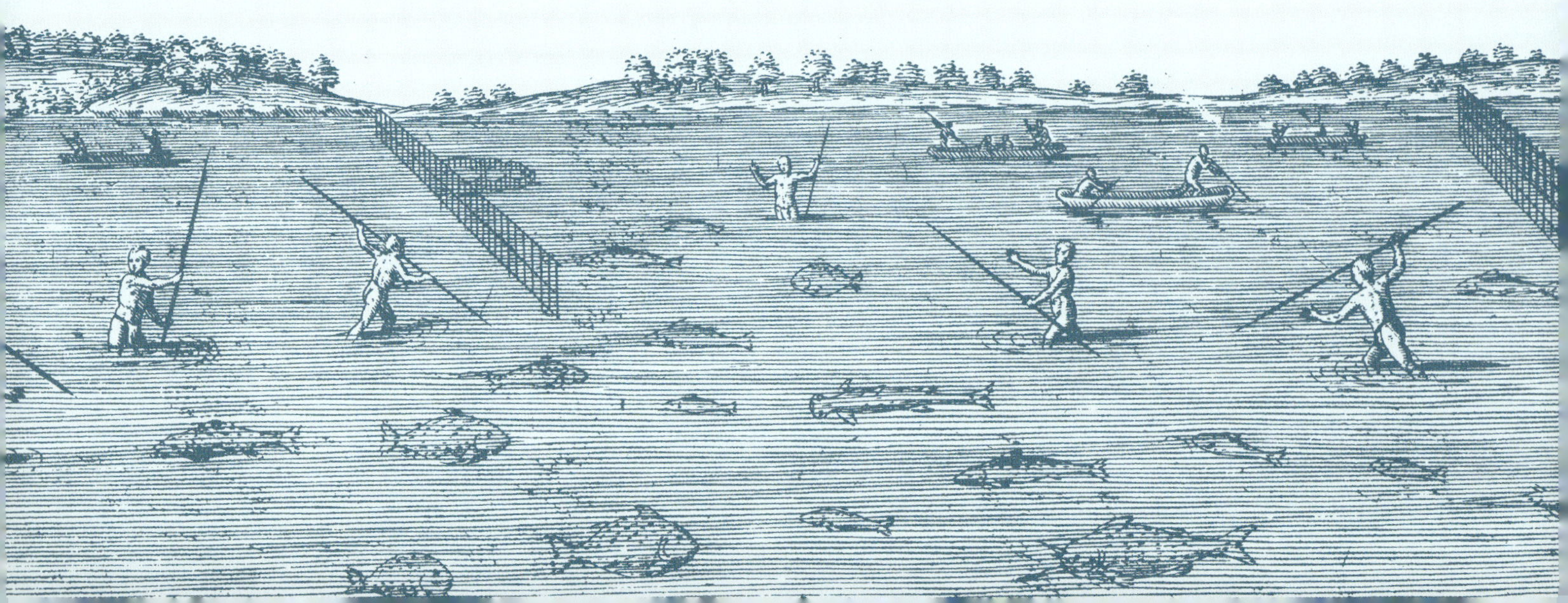

First Colony Foundation president—as well as lawyer and historian—Phil Evans begins this story of discovery. He describes the moment when the men, women, and children of Sir Walter Raleigh's colony, who had disembarked at Roanoke Island in 1587, were nowhere to be found in 1590. They left behind contradictory clues as to their destination but no sign that they were in danger. They had simply disappeared.

After Jamestown was founded in 1607, generations of Virginian explorers, trappers, and traders occasionally visited the deserted ruins on Roanoke and heard from Indians elsewhere stories of a few white people living in other parts. But no reliable evidence came to light during four centuries. Hopes were raised when the Dare Stones of the 1930s purported to mark the westward journey of the colony's leading family—but they were later proven to be fakes.

Phil explains how the Old Fort Raleigh site on Roanoke survived in memory, was then preserved as a historic park, and has been commemorated in an outdoor drama that is still performed throughout the summer months. Modern archaeology unearthed exciting evidence from the Elizabethan activities there, and renewed historical research continues to inform us about the colony and its colonists. Yet there was no new hard evidence—that is, until First Colony Foundation was formed in 2004 and soon began to reexamine the site, the records, and even Sir Walter's maps.

Figure 1.1. Theodor de Bry, *Arrival of the English*, 1590. Library of Congress.

chapter one

THE SEARCH FOR RALEIGH'S COLONY

Phillip W. Evans

Even before the sun rose over the Atlantic Coast at that part of Sir Walter Raleigh's Virginia, well known today as the Outer Banks of North Carolina, a day began that would be closely studied for over four centuries. It started with uncertainty, worry, and perplexing questions. Before that long summer day ended, even more and bigger questions were to be raised, one of them launching the greatest mystery in American history (fig. 1.1).

The single contemporary narrator of the day's events was John White, an English watercolor artist. He later prepared a fairly detailed account of what he saw and sent it in 1593 with a cover letter to Richard Hakluyt, a compiler of histories of English voyages. White had been appointed by Sir Walter Raleigh as governor of a colony bearing the name *The Cittie of Ralegh*. The group of English men, women, and children composing the colony had stopped at Roanoke Island slightly more than three years before, in late July 1587. The colonists included White's daughter, Eleanor, her husband, Ananias Dare, and their daughter, who had been born on the island exactly three years before on August 18, 1587. She had been christened with the name Virginia and is well remembered as the first English child born in the New World. White had departed Roanoke Island only a handful of days after the infant's baptism in 1587 but was not able to return until 1590, almost three years after he left. When he did return, in the two vessels that came to attack Spanish shipping in the West Indies, he brought no supplies and no additional colonists. At Roanoke, White may have hoped that some small party of the English or an English-friendly tribe could be found to give directions to the new "Cittie of Ralegh" settlement and information on what had happened during his absence. It was for this reason that White so assiduously pursued every sign of smoke he had seen on the shores of the barrier islands. The ships had just a few days before anchored at the east end of Croatoan Island (today's Hatteras). White and the sailors carefully measured the depth of the channel there but saw no smoke signal nor any sign of habitation on the near shore. Seeing nothing, they had sailed on up the barrier islands to Roanoke. If anyone—friend or foe—was at Croatoan, they had remained well hidden (fig. 1.2).

With all this on his mind, White spent the early morning of August 18, 1590, just off the north point of Roanoke Island. The sailors had spent several days sailing along the coast chasing what White seemed convinced were smoke signals from fires made on the sandy beaches and in

Figure 1.2. Detail of Outer Banks in map by Theodor de Bry of *Virginia*, 1590.

the coastal marshes. Were these fires at Roanoke really signals? Who was up at night and making them? Were these signs of friendly greeting or was there was something to fear on landing? White and the other men had called out and sung English songs in hopes of receiving a reply, but their efforts were met only with an almost haunting silence. White's landing party searched the north end of the island, finding a wooden palisade where houses and cottages of 1587 had stood. Those, White said, had been "taken down." At the entrance to the palisade was carved the word "CROATOAN." As evening approached, the search came to a close. No living person had been encountered, but neither had any bodies or graves. No cross, the agreed upon sign of distress, had been seen, yet that single Algonquian word was an enigmatic massage. White chose to interpret it to mean that he was to sail there to find them waiting for him, even though he had just been there and seen nothing. White and the sailors departed Roanoke Island, weather forcing them north, away from Croatoan, and no further search was made. Where had the colonists gone, why, and what had happened since 1587 was unknown. It still largely is. The puzzle pieces are few, small, and scattered by time.

Interest in locating the physical remains of Sir Walter Raleigh's colonies appeared shortly after hopes of finding any individuals from the colony founded in 1587 were extinguished. The English colonists at Jamestown, who first settled in 1607, did search for scattered survivors up through 1609, but the period of starvation known as the Starving Time at James Fort in the winter of 1609–10, wars between the English and the Powhatan Indians of Tidewater Virginia in the 1620s and 1640s, and the subsequent English expansion into areas inhabited by Powhatan allies delayed the colonists' return to Roanoke Island. Near the middle of the seventeenth century—sixty years after John White saw that his colony had left Roanoke—several Jamestown-area hunters, traders, and possible land speculators visited the island. They reported that they encountered a local Native hunting deer on the island who took them to the ruins of Sir Walter Raleigh's fort. One of the English later wrote that they secured "*a sure token*," or physical evidence, of earlier English presence there, but no one marked the colony site they visited on any map or described what they took from the site. A half-century later, around 1701, the English explorer John Lawson visited Roanoke. His description of what he saw was close to the one John White gave in 1590, but we cannot be sure where this was, and no one else ever described a site identical to it.

Another half-century passed on Roanoke Island without any description of remains of Raleigh's colonies, but it appears that local interest and perhaps memory focused on a site on the north end of the island. By 1768, mapmaker John Collet placed on a manuscript map of North Carolina and at the site of the present Fort Raleigh

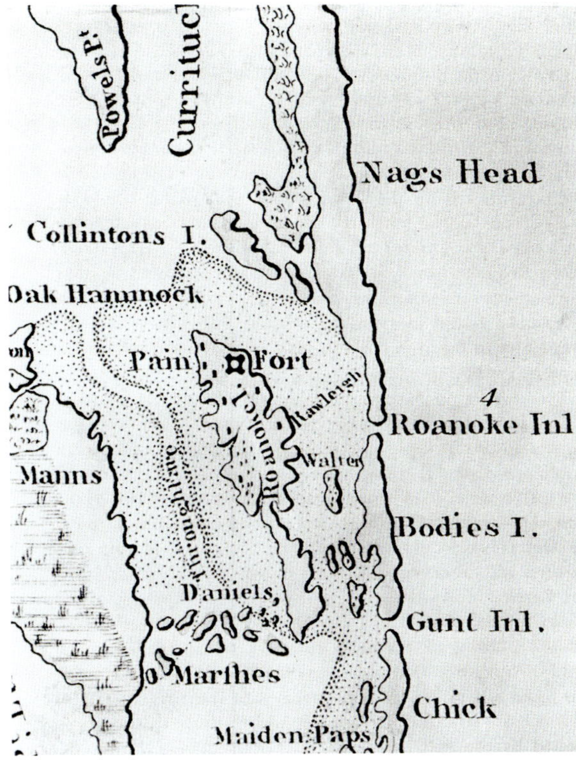

Figure 1.3. Detail of engraved map by John Collet of *North Carolina*, 1770. Wilson Library, University of North Carolina at Chapel Hill.

Figure 1.4. Monument to Sir Walter Raleigh's colonists, at "Old Fort Raleigh." National Park Service.

National Historic Site a traditional cartographer's fort symbol, adding notations of "Sr Walter, Raleigh," and "fort" (fig. 1.3).

By the time of the American Revolution, therefore, the area of the present Fort Raleigh was firmly associated in local history as a site of Raleigh's colonists. Earthwork of some sort of fort were still visible even though they had been diminished by time and the elements over two centuries. If any objects were found, removed, and retained by local inhabitants, they either do not survive or cannot be located today. Only the earthwork remains themselves were remarked on by early nineteenth-century writers, visited by President James Monroe in 1820, and cherished in local and state lore. After the American Civil War, North Carolina residents and expatriates became interest in preserving the earthwork site and making it a shrine to the Raleigh colonists. They purchased for preservation roughly sixteen acres of land and erected a stone monument (fig. 1.4). This "Old Fort Raleigh" quickly became a treasured and popular destination for visitors to coastal North Carolina. By 1921, interest was so high that a silent film was made at the fort site and distributed across the state to schools and communities where motion pictures were very new. Before then, however, archaeology had come to Roanoke Island in 1895 when Talcott Williams employed what was then the most advanced techniques of a pioneering discipline, digging test squares into the earthwork and at nearby sites believed to have evidence of Native American occupation.

After that, no archaeology at Roanoke Island was undertaken until the Fort Raleigh tract was made a unit of the National Park Service (NPS) in 1941. Even then archaeological research was delayed until the end of World War II. Before then, the Fort Raleigh tract was developed into a state historic attraction. Industrious tourism promotion centered in Dare County generated the building of a log palisade on top of the very diminished earthwork. Also constructed were several small log buildings that served for a small museum, a picturesque chapel, and a cottage to represent a dwelling of the colonists. At the edge of the property was a small concession stand that sold both refreshments and stones that the proprietor suggested had come from the ballast of Sir Walter Raleigh's ships. The year 1937 brought significant change to the site's shoreline when the producers of an outdoor drama, Paul Green's *The Lost Colony*, staged their production at a newly

Figure 1.5. A performance of the outdoor musical drama *The Lost Colony*. Courtesy of the Roanoke Island Historical Association. Roanoke Island Historical.

constructed venue, the Waterside Theatre, during the summer of the 350th anniversary of the birth of Virginia Dare (fig. 1.5). The show was a hit that benefited from a visit by President Franklin D. Roosevelt, but none of this activity at the site saw even the slightest archaeological examination before or after the excitement of 1937. In 1947, the NPS brought pioneering historical archaeologist Jean C. Harrington down from Jamestown, Virginia, to make a thorough and modern examination of Fort Raleigh. His work there from 1947 through 1950 was of the highest quality for his time and place, and it led to the reconstruction of the earthwork, both rampart and ditch.

Also in this postwar period, British historians undertook deep research into the publications of Richard Hakluyt in 1589 and 1600 as well as into records of the English admiralty. Foremost was David Beers Quinn, who in 1955 edited a two-volume work titled *The Roanoke Voyages* for the London-based Hakluyt Society. Following the lead of another London scholar, Kenneth R. Andrews, Quinn discovered that John White's last voyage to Roanoke Island was made in 1590, not 1591, as everyone who had read Hakluyt since 1600 assumed. Admiralty records detailing claims made in October 1590 by the privateering parties of the voyage and heard before an admiralty judge named Julius Caesar made clear that John White found the word "Croatoan" on August 18, 1590, and not a year later. This was unknown in 1937 when a hoaxer created the first Dare Stone and tried to pass it off during the 350th anniversary of the arrival of White's colony in 1587. Not knowing that the long-held 1591 date was wrong, the hoaxer carved the wrong date on the stone.

While Harrington was developing historical archaeology and investigating the sites of early English colonization at Jamestown and Roanoke Island there was little corresponding research into the Native Algonquians on the coast. Joffre Coe of the University of North Carolina and his colleagues carried out research in the Piedmont region, leading to the re-creation of a Native center at Town Creek Indian Mound in Montgomery County. But this was more than 200 miles from Roanoke and concerned very different times and cultures. It is not surprising that in the generation of Harrington and Coe, there was relatively little overlap of research interests, and the story of the Algonquians at Roanoke suffered. Over time, appreciation grew for the Native side of the Roanoke colonies story. In the 1960s, Fort Raleigh and *The Lost Colony* drama

Figure 1.6. Archaeologists Ivor Noël Hume (*left*) and J. C. Harrington (*right*), at the Fort Raleigh excavations in 1990–92. First Colony Foundation.

saw huge changes. The original 16 acres of the historic site were expanded to more than 100, a new and modern visitor center was built by the NPS to replace the little log cabin, and the top-level Broadway director Joe Layton was brought in to greatly improve the outdoor drama. Layton made many beneficial changes to costuming, dance, and staging, but he was not allowed to alter the original script of 1937. The Native actors continued to talk in what theater people called "Tonto," after the character in the television series *The Lone Ranger*.

The redevelopment of Fort Raleigh in the 1960s meant considerable digging and earth-moving to bring in modern utilities and allow for tourist access. In 1965, workers digging for a utility trench encountered early colonial brick and other artifacts, so the National Park Service brought Harrington out of retirement to excavate. Harrington did not interpret the remains beyond identifying the site as an outwork of the larger earthwork fort. In the 1980s, the NPS Southeast Archeological Center renewed excavation in the area of Harrington's outwork and west of the earthwork as part of the four-hundredth anniversary of the Roanoke colonies. But it did not result in any really satisfying interpretation of the remains. The work in the 1980s had been motivated in large part by the success of Colonial Williamsburg archaeologist Ivor Noël Hume in excavating and interpreting an English colonial settlement, Wolstenholme Town, circa 1620, near Jamestown. Some of the structural features found there were similar to what Harrington had found at Roanoke in 1965. When shown a diagram of the similarities, Harrington joked that it looked as if they had come from the same makers (fig. 1.6). In 1990 and 1992, Noël Hume directed excavations in and around the Fort Raleigh earthwork, identifying it as a scientific workshop associated with the first Roanoke colony of 1585–86. Artifacts included metallurgical crucibles, laboratory glass, and other residue of testing on the site. The bricks were interpreted as pieces of the metallurgical furnace operated by a Joachim Gans, a Jewish native of Prague and expert on copper assay that Raleigh had recruited to join the colony. Leading the scientific work was the English polymath Thomas Harriot, who assessed the resource of the newly explored "Virginia." While Noël Hume's interpretation of the outwork was a resounding success, it was also a disappointment to the sponsoring National Geographic Society. It had been hoped that the excavations would uncover the still unidentified settlement of the English colonists. More work was needed, but there was no clue to where to dig next.

Alongside the successful excavations at Roanoke, great strides in the study of the Algonquian and Tuscarora peoples were made by East Carolina University's David Phelps. A solid foundational understanding of the region's Natives, including their village distributions, burials, and subsistence patterns, emerged to reflect the ethnological observations made by Thomas Harriot in the 1580s. After that, the late 1990s was a time with little archaeological or historical research regarding the Roanoke colonies. Ivor Noël Hume and David Phelps retired from field research. David Quinn entered that phase where one begins to exit life's stage. Public support waned in the years following the four-hundredth anniversary of the colonies. Noël Hume and Phelps had represented new thinking, where historical archaeologists and prehistorians freely shared information and perspectives. Perhaps equally important was the development by both men of a cadre of talented professional researchers—Nick Luccketti, Eric Klingelhofer, Clay Swindell, and others—who have continued to build the story into the twenty-first century. In 2004, members of the archaeological team from 1990–91 met at the University of North Carolina's Wilson Library to organize a research group dedicated to the long-term investigation of the Roanoke colonies, and all were delighted to have join them former UNC president William Friday and North Carolina historian William S. Powell. The terrestrial archaeologists soon invited North Carolina's leading maritime archaeologist, Gordon Watts, into the team. The group agreed to incorporate under the name First Colony Foundation (FCF), and I was chosen as its president. We planned to begin research as soon as funding could be secured. In 2005, the Walter A. Bloedorn Foundation of Washington, DC, made the first grant, and the foundation has been a faithful supporter over the years. The first fieldwork was underwater exploration conducted by Gordon Watts at Roanoke Island. Work went ashore in 2006 at Fort Raleigh near where I, then a National Park Service ranger, had in 1982 found the remains of what was determined to be an Elizabethan era barrel used as the interior lining for a well and, nearby, a more intact hollow log that had served the same purpose. These finds were made east of the Waterside Theatre on a shore of Roanoke Sound that was, and still is, suffering severe coastal erosion. On the bluff overlooking what we dubbed Barrel Beach, First Colony Foundation dug test units to rescue any archaeological remains before nature's carving knife sliced them away. Since then, the foundation has monitored coastal erosion both on park property and at the Elizabethan Gardens, an elaborate formal gardens created in the 1950s by the Garden Clubs of North Carolina as a memorial to the Raleigh era colonists, another area with high potential for Elizabethan remains. After 2006, attention turned to resolving the question of whether evidence of any additional Elizabethan structures existed around the earthwork fort and scientific workshop. The foundation was able to use the services of a remote sensing company, Witten Technologies, and in three years the two acres around the reconstructed fort were thoroughly examined by ground-penetrating radar, with tomographic imaging providing 3-D views, much like a sonogram. Likely anomalies noted in the virtual excavation were tested by real excavation, and all proved to be tree holes or the results of state park and national park operations. No one could find the colonists' settlement there because it was never there. The earthwork and the testing of natural resources had been placed some distance from the settlement.

At the same time, First Colony Foundation began fieldwork in the wooded dunes west of the earthwork in the area that the park service designates the Thomas Harriot Nature Trail. Test units in the mid-1990s suggested cultural remains in the area, so work was scheduled in 2008. The first

Figure 1.7. First Colony Foundation researchers soon after the British Museum map discovery. *Seated:* James Horn, Eric Klingelhofer. *Standing:* Brent Lane, Phil Evans, Nick Luccketti. Photo by Briana Brough for the *New York Times*, May 3, 2012.

week saw the participation of the public television production of a debuting archaeology series titled *Time Team America*. The second week followed with less fanfare but more interesting finds. A complete copper necklace that was likely made by the English to be given to the Roanoke leader was found in association with Italian glass beads. Work resumed along the nature trail in 2009 and 2010 with similar results: good artifacts but scant evidence of buried archaeological features. The time had come to pause fieldwork to digest several dig seasons. Meanwhile, the NPS went forward with a badly needed renewal of the visitor center museum, designing its exhibition around the archaeological research at Fort Raleigh. While First Colony Foundation people were consulting with the NPS on this and assessing the finds from 2008 to 2010, underwater archaeologist Watts explored the submerged areas off the park beach. His study indicates that although shoreline erosion is a real problem, not as much shore has been lost as some have postulated, and the survival of at least part of the Elizabethan fort and settlement remains a possibility.

Before a remarkable discovery in 2012 at the British Museum in London, all eyes were focused on Roanoke Island and Croatoan on Hatteras Island, where colonists and Algonquians were known to have been active. That discovery came, not from looking into the mainland for a site related to the Lost Colony of 1587, but from quite separate research to determine where along the Pamlico Sound had stood the town of Secotan, shown in 1585 on John White's watercolor map of Virginia and in 1590 on Theodor de Bry's engraving of that map. Through the interest of leaders in Beaufort County, FCF had undertaken to study a variety of evidence to narrow down the site of Secotan. Clay Swindell combined historical records and archaeological field reports of Late Woodland Period (800–1650 CE) sites with map locations of soil types where crops important to the Algonquians could be grown successfully. Two areas on separate watercourses seemed to fit all the essential requirements. One was the west bank of lower Bath Creek across from the colonial townsite of 1705. The other was the west bank of the Pungo River south of Belhaven and near the locality known for at least two centuries as Woodstock. But how well did this analysis fit with the early maps of John White and Theodor de Bry? This question became a special interest of Brent Lane, then an FCF board member. Familiar with the north shore of the Pamlico from having spent some time there in geological and geographic study, he saw things in the early maps that could only have been learned by a person who was there for a good bit of time or by a skilled team of careful observers spread over the wide area. Noticeable on the watercolor map but unstudied and scarcely mentioned in earlier studies are places where small pieces of paper were applied to the surface of the underlying map surface. On the piece applied in the area along the Pamlico, watercolor that appears to be corrective of the original depiction of the shoreline was added to the upper surface of the small paper piece. This was the area of interest for FCF because it is where Secotan was located.

In November 2011, some of us gathered in Chapel Hill at UNC's Kenan-Flagler Business School, where Brent Lane worked, while others participated by phone (fig. 1.7). The subject of the meeting was to plan the next year's research. We wanted to review the work Clay Swindell had done to identify possible sites for Secotan and determine whether excavations in Beaufort County were possible. Because Theodor de Bry's print of Secotan had become the essential "Indian village" to the world, its importance cannot be overstated. But we did not know whether Beaufort County would continue to support research or if landowners would allow access to their properties. We also considered possible sites on Roanoke Island outside the boundaries of Fort Raleigh National Historic Site. Foundation archaeologist Eric Deetz had already directed a small dig where an Elizabethan coin had once been found well off NPS property. Although the results were not positive, it was near an area where in the 1890s Talcott Williams had found a sand hill containing multiple Native burials. It was also near a local landmark called Indian Hole that David Phelps had partially examined. All this was pondered as the meeting ended late on that cloudy and blustery November afternoon. Acceptable to everyone was a plan that Brent Lane would ask the British Museum what lay under the patch on the map. We extended best wishes for the upcoming Thanksgiving holiday and resolved to await whatever news came from Roanoke, the Pamlico, or even London.

part two

FIRST COLONY FOUNDATION ENTERS THE SEARCH

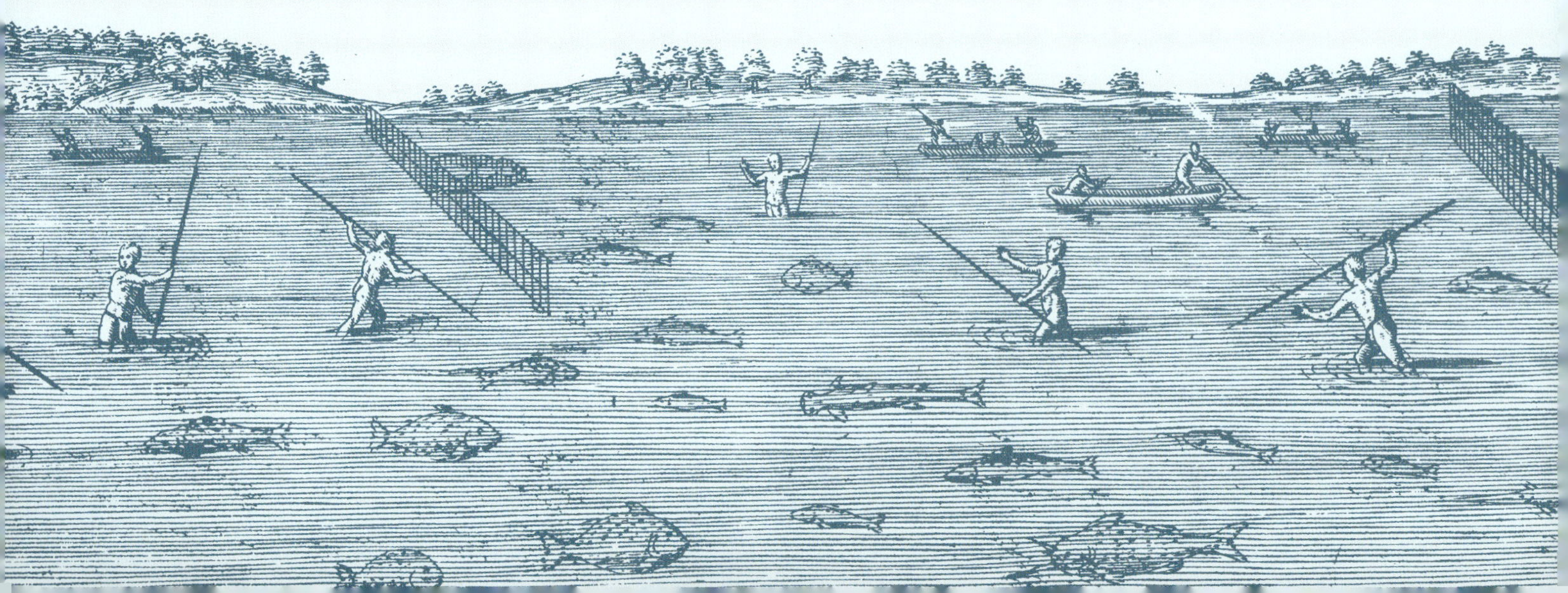

By 2012, First Colony Foundation had spent several seasons coming to understand the archaeology at Fort Raleigh and had begun to look beyond Roanoke Island. Ground-penetrating radar and "ground-truthing" by test excavation of its radar anomalies told us that there was little more to find around the earthwork itself, though what had been excavated previously could well yield more details and artifacts. The twentieth century had been harsh to the site. Access road grading sheared off some of the remnant earthwork, then landscaping for the state park's reconstructed village removed perhaps a foot of the original topsoil and the information it contained. Below today's wooded parkland, trenches for multiple utility lines cut through the site, and earlier excavations left little for more discerning eyes to find.

But to our minds, the negative evidence helped answer important questions. Raleigh's second expedition, in 1585, landed over 100 soldiers at Roanoke Island, where Captain Ralph Lane established a base camp comprising a wooden fort and adjacent lodgings. But Lane's fort and village was never at this site. As archaeologist Ivor Noël Hume had earlier determined, the small earthwork of "Old Fort Raleigh" had not been erected beside a settlement but by a workshop, where Thomas Harriot and Joachim Gans analyzed the botanical and mineral resources of their New Found World. There was positive evidence, too, both east and west of that site. The eroding shore below a modern bluff northeast of the earthwork held remnants of barrel wells. By matching previous topographic records and the existing geology, we estimated that the land had once sloped gently through a freshwater-bearing stratum to a possible cove or landing beach.

At the same time, First Colony Foundation archaeologists discovered that the acres of wooded dunes along the island's shore west of the earthwork had formed in the later 1700s and that the soil they buried contained scattered Elizabethan artifacts: small sherds of storage vessels and crucibles as well as trade beads. Under the dunes we also found two small pits dating to the late 1500s and containing a necklace of European diamond-shaped copper plates and a pile of beads from Venice. No doubt intended as gifts to local Indian leaders, these valuable items had been carefully buried, suggesting to us, first, that their burial was to safeguard them for a future use, and second, that much more—perhaps the colonists' settlement—could be found under the unexamined dunes.

Meanwhile, we ventured beyond Roanoke to Beaufort County in search of the important Algonquian tribal center of Secotan. Through John White's drawings and their later publication in Theodor de Bry's prints, Secotan became the archetypal Indian town for generations of Europeans. White's *La Virginea Pars* watercolor map in the British Museum, however, displayed some irregularity—a repair—near Secotan and another at a distant, northern location. Investigating these would lead the First Colony team in an unexpected direction.

The following three sections focus on John White's maps. They are written by the individuals who led complementary avenues of research. Kim Sloan of the British Museum narrates the story of how the hidden symbol was discovered and how the *Virginea Pars* map was altered. Peter Barber, formerly of the British Library, provides background information on Tudor mapmaking to explain the purpose of Raleigh's cartographic project. And my close inspection of John White's New World maps reveals undocumented details of the colony's expedition and exploration. Drawn from an unexpected and extraordinary windfall, these papers literally mark a new chapter in Roanoke Colony studies.

Figure 2.1a. View of the Department of Prints and Drawings, British Museum. Photo by author.

Figure 2.1b. An open Solander box containing some of the drawings by John White. Photo by author.

chapter two

PAPER PATCHES

La Virginea Pars Map in the British Museum

Kim Sloan

In 2007, the British Museum organized an exhibition of the drawings by the English artist John White, which are kept in the Department of Prints and Drawings (figs. 2.1a and 2.1b). The department has more than a million works on paper, and most of them fade if exposed to the light for very long, so none of the collection is on permanent display. Instead, rotating exhibitions of selections from the collection are put on in a large gallery in the museum, which also lends hundreds of drawings and prints to exhibitions around the world every year and sends entire exhibitions of works on tour. The exhibition held in 2007, *A New World: England's First View of America*, was one of these touring exhibitions, and after it was shown at the British Museum, it traveled to the North Carolina Museum of History in Raleigh, the Yale Center for British Art in New Haven, Connecticut, and the Jamestown Settlement in Virginia. Afterward, the drawings returned to their boxes in the Prints and Drawings Study Room, where they can be seen by appointment.

As the curator of the British school in this, the national collection of works on paper, I was responsible for this exhibition. The John White drawings, dating from 1585 to 1586, are some of the earliest works in the collection, and we have to be very careful not to lend them too often or too long, as they will fade. Because the museum had been receiving an increasing number of requests for these works in the 1990s and been turning them down because the same ones were requested to be borrowed again and again, it was decided to do one big touring exhibition of them all and then let them rest for a decade or so.

In 2004, I traveled to the University of North Carolina and to Roanoke Island to do research that informed the book that accompanied the exhibition, published by the British Museum and UNC Press. At a conference at the British Museum, experts discussed the drawings, their subjects, and their influence on Europeans. The proceedings were published in 2009 under the title *European Visions: American Voices*, which is available online through the National Archives website (for both publications, see "Further Readings").

But then several years later, in January 2012, FCF board member Brent Lane wrote to one of my colleagues, Alice Rugheimer, a paper conservator who had published on the drawings in the conference proceedings. He explained that the foundation was doing research on the village of Secotan and had noticed two patches on the map, and he wanted to know whether they obscured any other imagery (fig. 2.2). It took a bit of time

Figure 2.2. John White (fl. 1585–93), *Map of La Virginea Pars*, ca. 1585. Pen and ink with watercolor, gold, and silver. British Museum, Dept. of Prints and Drawings, 1906,0509.1.3. © The Trustees of the British Museum.

before Alice and I could get to it, but on February 24, we managed to get the map out and put it on a light box in the old paper conservation studio (fig. 2.3). We looked very carefully at the patch that has the village of Secotan on it and noted a few changes in the coastline (figs. 2.4 and 2.5), but then we took a quick look at a second patch higher up, not expecting anything (fig. 2.6). We quickly saw there was actually something very substantial there, and looking very closely, I could see that the marking resembled what I recognized to be the symbol for a fort (fig. 2.7). I said to Alice, "I think we just discovered the intended site for the 'Cittie of Ralegh,' the colony that John White was sent to Virginia to found." And then I think I swore. Not perhaps the reaction you might expect, but I had immediately realized how important this discovery might be to Americans, and especially to the people of North Carolina, and, at the same time, how much of my time answering questions about it, to which I didn't have the answers, was going to be taken up over the next few months, if not years.

The first question everyone asks is, "Is this the site of the Lost Colony?"—which of course I cannot answer. But the other most common question is, "How did you make the discovery?" Once they learn how simple it was, they ask, "Why did no one do this before?"

To answer these questions, it is important to know the history of the drawings, where they have been and how they have been kept over the 400 years since they were made. But even then, there are many unanswered questions. The title page still in the album where the drawings were once kept said that the pictures were "of sondry things collected and counterfeited according to the truth" in the voyage made in 1585 (see fig. 2.15). This was the second voyage to North America, during which Thomas Harriot and John White were tasked with making maps of the coastline: Harriot with the navigational and cartographic skills and White with the ability to record his findings. Peter Barber's essay in this

Figure 2.3. (*top*) *Map of La Virginea Pars*, placed on a light box. Photo by author.

Figure 2.4. (*middle*) John White, *Map of La Virginea Pars*, ca. 1585. Detail of the patch on the area around Secotan. Photo by author.

Figure 2.5. (*bottom*) The same detail as figure 2.4, seen on a light box. Photo by author.

Figure 2.6. (*top*) John White, *Map of La Virginea Pars*, ca. 1585. Detail of the patch on the area around Weapemeoc. © The Trustees of the British Museum.

Figure 2.7. (*bottom*) The same detail as figure 2.6, seen on a light box. Photo by author.

volume provides more information about the details of this voyage.

When organizing the exhibition, I had asked my colleague Janet Ambers from the scientific research department to do a technical analysis of the pigments used in order to see if any of them might have been made using local earths or minerals in North Carolina—in other words drawn, on the spot—or whether John White used pigments that were from Europe, either bringing them with him or making the drawings once he returned. She couldn't remove any flakes of pigment, so she used two noninvasive, nondestructive methods: X-ray fluorescence, which uses helium gas and X-rays to give details of the elements present on the surface, and Raman spectroscopy, which uses lasers to collect spectra from a sample only a few micrometers in size to identify the chemical compounds present. She also examined the surfaces with optical microscopy. Her report is published in the conference proceedings and available as a free downloadable pdf on the National Archives website (see "Further Readings"). She found that the pigments were what we would expect of any drawings made in Europe at the time, including vermilion, indigo and two other types of blue, yellow ocher, gum for binding, carbon black, graphite, and a sap green that is mostly badly faded. She concluded that overall the palette is typical of its period and that none of these pigments are specific to the Americas, so we know that White did not collect them there. But this still doesn't help us to answer whether he produced them on the spot or after his return.

Janet Ambers did tell us two things, however, that help us to see the artwork in a different light. One was that White used a lead white pigment, which discolors over time, so that many of the spots that are now black or gray were once bright white (fig. 2.8). The beads on the necklaces and the whites of the eyes, for example, were originally white, which means that the beads were not black pearls or shells, as they have often been described, but large white pearls of great value to the Elizabethan viewers and that the faces of the people with white eyeballs would have looked much less strange and alien than they do to us now that they are discolored black.

The other point Janet Ambers made in her article was about John White's use of gold and silver in his pictures. Fish, for example, when they are alive, are iridescent, and in order to capture this, John White used these precious pigments, and the effect he was aiming for can be restored digitally. This is quite different from what we see now, streaks of gray on the bellies and black in the center of the gold eyes, instead of white surrounding the black pupils. Gold and silver were also found in the drawings of the North Carolina Algonquians. Nicholas Hilliard, Queen Elizabeth I's official limner, wrote a well-known treatise on miniature painting, known as limning, which reveals that it was common for miniaturists at the time to use gold and silver in their works to catch the light and add to the precious quality of their images. John White used it in the flames of the fires in his drawings (fig. 2.9) and, in figure 2.8, the young girl is showing her mother a gold coin on a red necklace, and her doll also had gold on her hat—both of these objects with gold are gifts from the English colonists.

The effect of all of these changes on how we now see John White's pictures is minor compared to the disaster that befell them in 1865. We don't know how they were kept on White's return in 1586 when they were used to drum up support at court and among the merchant adventurers for Raleigh's next venture, a civilian colony, but we can presume that at some point the drawings were put in an album. That was how they were sold in 1788 in what was described as the original folio binding when the Earl of Charlemont purchased them for fourteen guineas at an auction in London. They were probably still in the same album when his descendants consigned them to Sotheby's Auction House in 1865. Unfortunately, the album was in Sotheby's warehouse when an

Figure 2.8. John White, *A Wife of an Indian Werowance and Her Daughter*, ca. 1585. Watercolor and bodycolor with white and gold. British Museum, Dept. of Prints and Drawings, 1906,0509.1.13. © The Trustees of the British Museum.

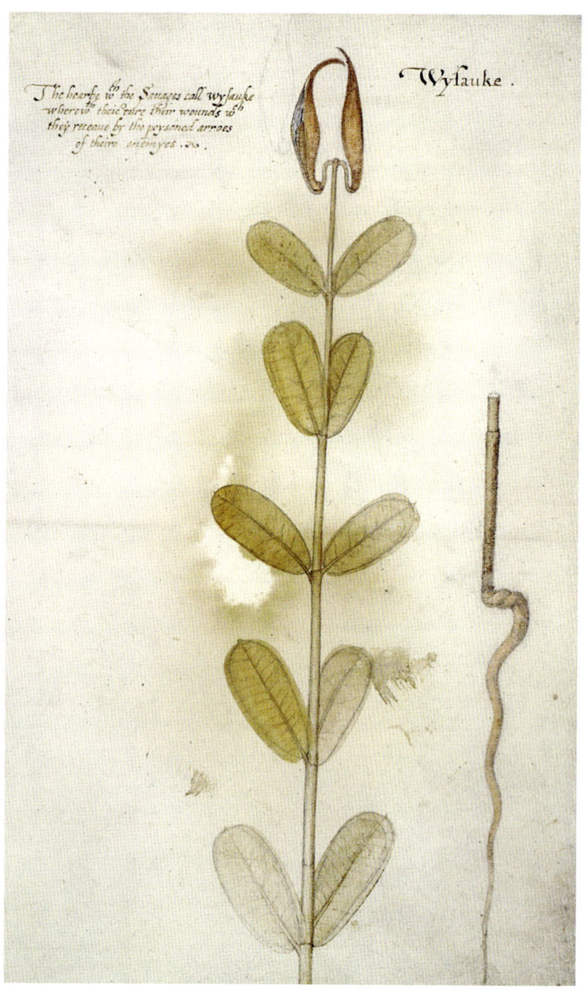

adjoining warehouse caught fire, scorching the book's spine. The album was doused with water and then lay compressed under other books for three weeks before it was salvaged and consigned for sale. It is that damage that appears in so many of the drawings and is especially clear in the drawing of the Wysauke (fig. 2.10). The album was then purchased by Henry Stevens of Vermont for 125 pounds, and he had the drawings removed and placed in a new album and then sold them to the British Museum (fig. 2.11). There, they were placed in the printed books library, alongside the publication with the engravings after them by Theodor de Bry—*A briefe and true report of the new found land of Virginia* (1590). In 1907, they moved from the book library to the Department of Prints and Drawings as examples of important early English watercolors.

While damp and under pressure in 1865, the pigments were offset onto the interleaved sheets of paper that had been previously inserted into the album to protect the drawings and now acted like blotting paper—it is an offset that one can see bound in a separate album (fig. 2.12). Given how much pigment went into the offset, one can imagine how much deeper and brighter the colors once were and how much crisper and better defined the original drawings had been before the fire. The reds and blacks suffered particularly.

Some of the larger drawings had been folded in half in the album and in this instance were offset onto the other half of the drawing, as is apparent in the image where ghostly extra limbs appear on the dancing figures (fig. 2.13). The maps were also folded within the album and suffered the same kind of damage. On the large map of the Caribbean Islands, where White had first landed, and off the coast of Florida, which the explorers followed up to Virginia, ghost images of a whale and ship appear on the left along with the compass and Raleigh's coat of arms (fig. 2.14). The map *La Virginea Pars* was folded, not in half, but instead down across the top third (see fig. 2.2).

The line running through the "V" and "I" was the fold, so the offset of the Chesapeake upper coastline running in pale blue appears just above the upper patch, and of course the offsets of the compass and of Queen Elizabeth's coat of arms show most clearly. Incidentally, there are traces of silver in the fuzells argent (silver diamonds) running across Raleigh's coat of arms (see fig. 2.4), and there is still some gold and silver in the queen's arms, which once showed the lions couchant and fleur-de-lis of her crest.

So this is what the First Colony Foundation team was viewing when they were researching the location of the village of Secotan, saw the patches, and Brent Lane asked us what might be underneath them. The paper conservator Alice Rugheimer and I knew that we couldn't lift the patches; they were glued down at the time the map was made or shortly afterward, and lifting them would destroy the map and anything underneath them. X-rays will show pencil or carbon underneath layers of paint but are no good for seeing through layers of paper. The only way to determine whether the drawing was different underneath the patches was very simple: by placing the drawing on a light table and then turning off the lighting in the room. What we saw under the larger patch that includes the village of Secotan (spelt "Secoton" on the map) was not much, but White appears to have sketched part of the coastline below the word "Seco" along a different line, and the patch covered this up (see figs 2.4 and 2.5). This fits entirely with what an artist had to do when he couldn't erase a mistake or cover it with other lines or paint; here, if White had drawn the new coast without other changes, there would be an incorrect extra line that might be confused for a river. He also seems to have changed his mind about the village locations. The village of Seco is marked by a faint circle farther south, just visible, and now covered by the patch, and the village of Secotaoc has also been moved to the west. So, he put a clean piece of paper on top to cover all his mistakes and redrew and

Figure 2.9. (*opposite, top*) John White, *A Fire Ceremony*, ca. 1585. Detail of the fire. Watercolor and bodycolor over black lead with white and gold. British Museum, Dept. of Prints and Drawings, 1906,0509.1.11. Photo by author.

Figure 2.10. (*opposite, bottom*) John White, *Wysauke*, ca. 1585. Watercolor over black lead. British Museum, Dept. of Prints and Drawings, 1906,0509.1.37. © The Trustees of the British Museum.

Figure 2.11. (*above*) The albums that contained John White's drawings and the offsets, as bound by Henry Stevens. Photo by author.

Figure 2.12. (*above*) The album of offsets from the John White drawings, open to the offset of the drawing of *A Wife of an Indian Werowance and Her Daughter*. Photo by author.

Figure 2.13. (*opposite*) John White, *A Festive Dance*, ca. 1585. Watercolor and bodycolor over black lead. British Museum, Dept. of Prints and Drawings, 1906,0509.1.10. © The Trustees of the British Museum.

colored that part, including where the patch had partly covered a ship.

Janet Ambers's detailed technical analyses were published in the British Museum Technical Bulletin (see "Further Readings"). She noted that in places White had corrected initial mistakes in graphite, such as in the coastline below Pomeioc, simply by ignoring and painting over them. The errors described here, however, could not be repaired merely by drawing the correct coastline or changing the village dots, so White placed new paper on top and redrew and recolored it.

Although the use of patches by artists is not frequent, they certainly do occur and are usually so skillfully done that they are barely noticeable. So the reason for the lower larger patch on White's map near Secotan was clear, but why had he placed the smaller one higher up? This patch clearly wasn't added to correct the coastline (see figs. 2.6 and 2.7). The patch doesn't even entirely cover the coast, but what it did cover was the symbol underneath and a small circle, possibly representing a village, as the other red dots on the map did. But unlike those villages, this one hadn't been labeled with a name. After enhancement of the images through various photo-imagining techniques, the evidence indicates that it is a symbol representing a fortified town or fortress. I leave it to the historians and map specialists to say what exactly the symbol represents. I point out, however, that the marking seems to me to be disproportionate in size and is certainly symbolic, like the two coats of arms of Raleigh and Elizabeth, to which it is almost comparable. Interestingly, before it was covered, the symbol would have been a large feature of the map, directly midway between the two coats of arms. The circle and the star shape, which appear to be red and blue, are clear in these images. What is also clear and has always been visible with the naked eye, though only in certain light, is the impression of another drawing of a similar star-shaped form on the top of the patch (see fig. 2.6). This one appears to include a double outer wall

as well. And it is worth recalling that the line that runs horizontally through it is where the map was folded in the album.

Janet Ambers did further studies on this upper drawing on top of the patch. It is not in graphite or watercolor, nor does it leave an indentation in the paper, which means that the medium was liquid and applied with a brush. Her tests could reveal something only if the medium was mineral, and she determined that it was organic. She speculated that the drawing might have been made with something intended to remain invisible until it was heated or lit in a special way, such as alum, milk, citrus juice, or even urine, all of which were then in use as invisible ink. But she concluded that it could equally have been drawn in something that was actually visible at the time but has now faded. Neither of us felt that there was enough evidence here to conclude anything, only to speculate.

But why had no one mentioned the symbol on top or simply placed the drawing on a light table to look at what was under the patches before we were asked by First Colony Foundation in 2012? We can't, of course, say for certain, but the answer is again relatively simple and lies in the history of the album and how the drawings were stored and exhibited in the twentieth century according to the museum's standard practices (fig. 2.15). When the drawings were in private hands through the eighteenth and nineteenth centuries, they were stuck down in an album to be shown to friends as curiosities. After Stevens sold them to the British Museum, they remained in an album and sat on the library shelves with the printed books, not a place

Figure 2.14. John White, *La Virgenia Pars (map of East Coast of North America, including the Caribbean)*, ca. 1585. Pen and ink over black lead, with watercolor, white silver, and gold. British Museum, Dept. of Prints and Drawings, 1906,0509.1.2. © The Trustees of the British Museum.

where drawings were usually kept or studied. When they came to the drawings department, they were still in the album that Stevens had put them in, and the map *La Virginea Pars* was stuck down and folded across the top. White's drawings remained in the album until they were removed for an exhibition in 1965 that toured in Washington, DC, the North Carolina Museum of Art in Raleigh, and New York's Pierpont Morgan Library, when they were mounted in the standard way that the museum had kept individual drawings since the 1840s, which was to be guarded down on solid cream mounts with large margins for handling them in the acid-free boxes in which they are stored on the shelves in the study room (see fig. 2.1). On exhibition, they were simply placed in standard-sized

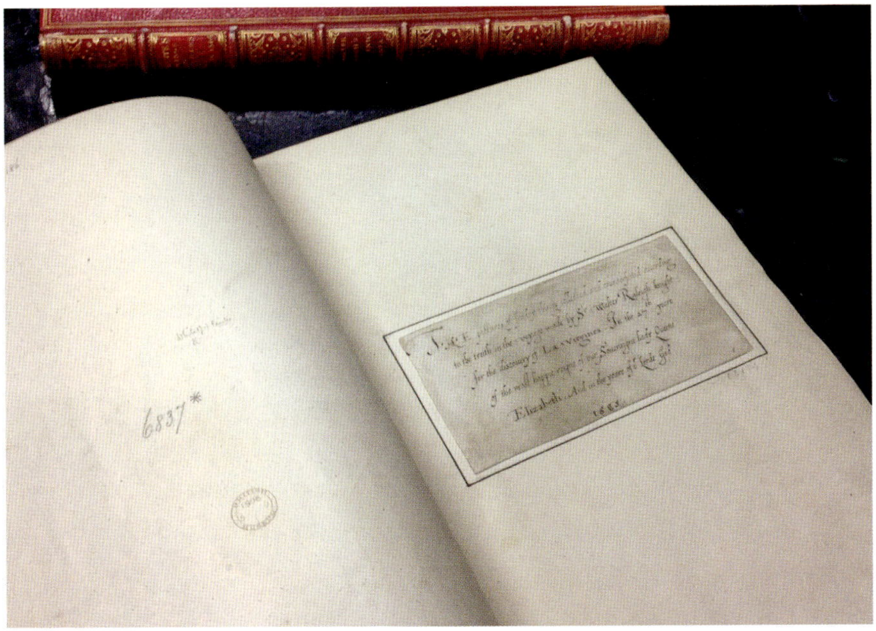

Figure 2.15. The album that once contained the John White drawings, open to the title page still mounted in the album. British Museum, Dept. of Prints and Drawings, 1906,0509.1.1. Photo by author.

frames. They were exhibited in this manner by the British Library in 1984 and then toured the United States again in 1985, traveling once more to Raleigh, this time to the North Carolina Museum of History, and to the New York Public Library. Several were shown at the Royal Maritime Museum in Greenwich in an exhibition on Elizabeth I in 2003.

Until preparations for the exhibition of 2007, there was no opportunity for anyone to see the back of the drawings or hold them up to the light. Some of the drawings were cockling or pulling on the guarded mounts, so we decided to remount them using inlays (each drawing is inserted into a precut window in a sheet of acid-free paper of similar weight), an expensive and time-consuming process that is undertaken only for exhibitions. While the drawings were being remounted, I was focused on their surfaces, asking Janet to examine the pigments. Her colleagues also assessed the fire and water damage to the drawings and the evidence of the offsets. None of us had a reason to put them on a light box—we were focused on those technical issues and on getting them remounted in time for the exhibition. When the exhibition tour was finished, they simply went back into their boxes, and I began work on three other exhibitions. There the map *La Virginea Pars* remained—until, that is, Brent Lane wrote on behalf of First Colony Foundation to ask about the patches. With the map now inlaid and not stuck down, we were easily able to slit the hinges that held it in the mount and to place the map on the light table. The rest, as they say, is history.

Sadly, Janet Ambers suffered a stroke not long after her analysis of the White drawings was completed, and she died in 2017. She enjoyed working on the map and was excited by the discoveries, but at one point, inundated with requests for information about it and desperately trying to meet other deadlines, she had written to me—I can just see her wry grin—asking, "Can't we just say we've lost it?" Yes, it added to our workloads, but working on the John White drawings has been a wonderful, exciting, and most rewarding journey, full of questions that I still cannot answer. Yet this is the best kind of historical quest, one that just keeps asking us to try to find further truths about the past in order to learn from it for the future.

BRITISH
MUSEUM

chapter three

JOHN WHITE'S MAPS AND TUDOR CARTOGRAPHY

Peter Barber

Before 1528, four principal types of maps existed in western Europe: medieval world maps, maritime charts, Ptolemaic maps for teaching history, and lawyers' sketch maps. And these types did not entirely disappear over the subsequent decades of what has been called the cartographic revolution of the sixteenth century. Perhaps the best known of these are the encyclopedic, symbolic, and devotional world maps called *mappae mundi*. Such maps included theological, ethnographical, botanical, zoological, and historical features in addition to geographical elements, which were subordinated to the other categories of information. These continued to be created long after the heyday of the great mural maps in around 1300. The so-called Psalter map of about 1265 in the British Library is a good example of a mappa mundi (see figs. 3.1a and 3.1b).

Figure 3.1a. (*opposite*) The "Psalter" world map, Westminster, ca. 1265. BL Add MS 28681. © The British Library Board.

Figure 3.1b. (*above*) Detail showing supposed peoples of the Indies. BL Add MS 28681. © The British Library Board.

The sea chart, or portolan, was a map meant for practical navigational and planning purposes. Portolans are much more recognizable as maps to the modern eye. They are generally believed to have originated in the western Mediterranean in about 1100, though the earliest extant example dates from about 1280. Initially confined to the Mediterranean and Black Seas, by the sixteenth century sea charts had spread to the known world.

Figure 3.2a. (*top*) This map depicting part of Dorset on the south coast of England dates from 1539, when there was a serious threat of French invasion. Though pictorial, the map exaggerates the size of the beaches—where landings were most likely to take place—which are shown in pink. It reduces the size of cliffs where landings were unlikely, and it highlights the beacons that would be lit to summon help should there be an enemy landing. BL Cotton Augustus I.i.31,33. © The British Library Board.

Figure 3.2b. (*bottom*) *Newe Haven.* Detail of an anonymous English plan of Le Havre with an arrow indicating the now detached and pasted down flap containing proposals for its refortification, ca. 1563. BL Cotton MS Augustus I.ii.78. © The British Library Board.

Ptolemaic maps, which became especially popular among those with intellectual pretensions after 1400, originated in copies of Claudius Ptolemy's *Geographia*. The outlines, based on text and geometric coordinates set out in about 150 CE, had been brought to Rome shortly after 1400, when Ptolemy's work was translated from Greek into Latin. Strikingly different in appearance to mappae mundi, these maps depicted the classical world and were recommended as a means of teaching history to the young. As early as the 1430s, these maps were seen to be defective, and "modern" Ptolemaic maps were created in increasing numbers to correct errors and incorporate the latest knowledge and discoveries. John White's regional maps belong to this group.

Maps created for utilitarian, purposes are common today—albeit often in electronic form—but unlikely as it may seem, few medieval Europeans grasped that maps could be of practical use. Utilitarian maps were not completely unknown in the Middle Ages, however. From about 1400 increasing numbers were created, often as sketch maps by lawyers trying to get a better understanding of their cases by depicting them graphically.

English Mapmaking in the Sixteenth Century

In the course of the sixteenth century, lawyers, who had been drawing and using utilitarian maps, became essential cogs in the machinery of government of modernizing western European states. The influence of such lawyers-turned-administrators may in part explain why, from the late 1520s, the value of maps as utilitarian planning tools and aids to government became more widely appreciated. From the mid-sixteenth century the variety and number of such maps expanded dramatically in England.

But what did these new maps look like, and what were they used for? Their appearance varied greatly, because a variety of techniques were used. Some maps were drawn to a uniform mathematical scale (and sometimes in plan). Others were drawn in proportion but not to scale, and still others were more like pictures, to no uniform scale. The nature and appearance of these utilitarian maps were dictated by their intended purpose.

Many English maps were meant for military planning, which would apply to national defense, fortification, field campaigns, or siege operations. In 1539, at a time when invasion was a real possibility, a concerted effort was made to map the coasts of England and Wales, Calais, and the border with Scotland. Several of these maps survive (fig. 3.2a). Later, in the 1570s, 1580s, and 1590s, an attempt was made to repeat the exercise. More usually maps were used for improving England's defense installations, and there are numerous plans of fortresses and harbors with suggested improvements indicated, sometimes by flaps illustrating the improvements and sometimes by different colors (fig. 3.2b). In many cases, though, to the confusion of future historians, no distinction was made between the old and the proposed, because the plan was meant for direct discussion among the decision makers. In a similar way, maps and plans were increasingly used to keep king or queen and ministers informed about the progress of sieges and to win their approval for measures that needed to be taken.

In addition to military maps, the sixteenth century saw the new cartography put to other

Figure 3.3. John Rogers, map of surroundings of Boulogne, with a dotted red line, possibly inserted by Henry VIII showing the preferred border with France, 1546. Cotton MS Augustus I.ii.77. © The British Library Board.

governmental purposes: diplomacy, administration, and surveys of national resources. Maps were increasingly used to define possible political boundaries (fig. 3.3). Maps were also becoming essential long-term reference tools, which is why the English government tried, as far as its finances permitted, to create reliable, relatively detailed national maps of the counties of England and Wales. This work was undertaken by Christopher Saxton in the 1570s. Some copies of these maps, and manuscript maps of the regions, were annotated by ministers of state, such as Lord Burghley, to indicate the homes of possible traitors and of loyal squires who could act as the eyes and ears of the Queen Elizabeth and her ministers in the provinces (fig. 3.4).

Maps also continued to be used to give information to the high and mighty about the latest geographical discoveries and their implications for trade. Last, when dealing with the wider—but still wealthy and influential—elites beyond the

Figure 3.4. Detail from Lord Burghley's copy of Saxton's map of Hertfordshire, with annotations in his hand giving the names of prominent gentry below their homes. BL Royal MS 18.D. III, ff. 33v–34. © The British Library Board.

royal court, there was the continuing need to educate, to commemorate, and to make propaganda, since maps were often displayed side by side with paintings and tapestries in the galleries of their spacious homes (fig. 3.5).

Working maps were often rough and sketchy (fig. 3.6a). But if intended for a powerful person from whom the supplicant and the mapmaker might obtain future favors or commissions, then the maps could be precisely drawn and very handsome, even if their purpose was relatively mundane (fig. 3.6b). Throughout the later sixteenth century, English mapmakers sought to assert that they were as good as, if not better than, their foreign counterparts in terms of the quality and scientific accuracy of their work. Their creations, in the form of globes, large wall maps, sheet maps, and atlases prove their case. Yet throughout the Tudor period, except for the decade between 1583 and 1593, the English lacked the technology to print from large plates, and almost all maps were sent to the Netherlands to be printed.

The Virginia Colony's Maps in Context

John White described in a letter of 1593 how, on his arrival on Roanoke for what proved to be his final visit in 1590, he had found the frames of his maps as well as drawings "rotten and spoiled with rain," scattered on the ground. The implication is that he had produced numerous maps, certainly many more than have survived. The words also remind us that maps at that time were as much decorative objects as practical aids. Maps with much the same content could serve utilitarian, decorative, scholarly, or propaganda purposes.

The surviving maps associated with Raleigh's Virginia colony fall into three categories. Some provided information on progress, to be used for supervision and planning from afar, including for purposes of defense against the Native inhabitants but particularly against a possible Spanish attack. Others met the requirements of instructions and provided Raleigh and the other backers with the privileged geographical, ethnographic, and cultural information that they craved. And there were those, mostly produced subsequently, that provided much the same information, generally for a wider readership, and served as propaganda for the achievements of Raleigh and the English.

Falling into the first category—and the only undoubted genuine survivor of this group—is the sketch map of the Outer Banks and the hinterland, more likely by Ralph Lane rather than John White, which was enclosed with Lane's dispatch to Elizabeth's minister Francis Walsingham of September 8, 1585, at the time of the first landings (fig. 3.7). It is very similar in appearance to other English Elizabethan sketch maps such as the one discussed above, by Sir Thomas Bodley, the commander of the English forces engaged in besieging the Spanish-held fortress of Groningen, in the Netherlands, in 1593. Simple and lacking in mathematical precision though it is, Lane's or White's sketch map would have been enough to keep Raleigh and the other backers of the project abreast of progress. It enabled them, in a rough and ready fashion, to ascertain the general situation and to guide the activities of the colonists. Included in this category would have been other maps and the plans of forts—initially sketchy but, when time allowed, like the sketch map of September 1585, compiled to create maps of larger areas, redrawn and elegantly finished, so as to appeal to the aesthetic as well as practical

Figure 3.5. Commemoration and propaganda for the people combined in this decorative map of 1590 by Jodocus Hondius linking Queen Elizabeth with her people and with her kingdom. BL 1175 (21). © The British Library Board.

sensibilities of Raleigh and his colleagues. Eventually, in 1590, the finished version of the sketch map from September 1585 was published by Theodor de Bry in embellished form under the title *The arrival of the Englishemen in Virginia* (see fig. 1.1).

The next type were the maps created in response to written instructions. These maps supplied the hard geographical information that Raleigh, his backers, and the Crown wished to garner from their expenditure in addition to the prestige of being associated with a patriotic colonial enterprise. There can be little doubt that before setting out, Thomas Harriot and John White received very detailed instructions as to the information they were to provide and particularly the nature of the maps they were expected to prepare. Though White's and Harriot's instructions are now lost, it seems generally accepted that they resembled the detailed instructions issued to Thomas Bavin, the artist-surveyor with Humphrey Gilbert's northern voyage of 1582. Bavin was not simply told in great detail about the geographical, physical ethnographical, zoological, and botanical phenomena that he should depict in his drawings. He was also instructed about the precise geographical signs he should use on his maps. Bavin's instructions reveal the

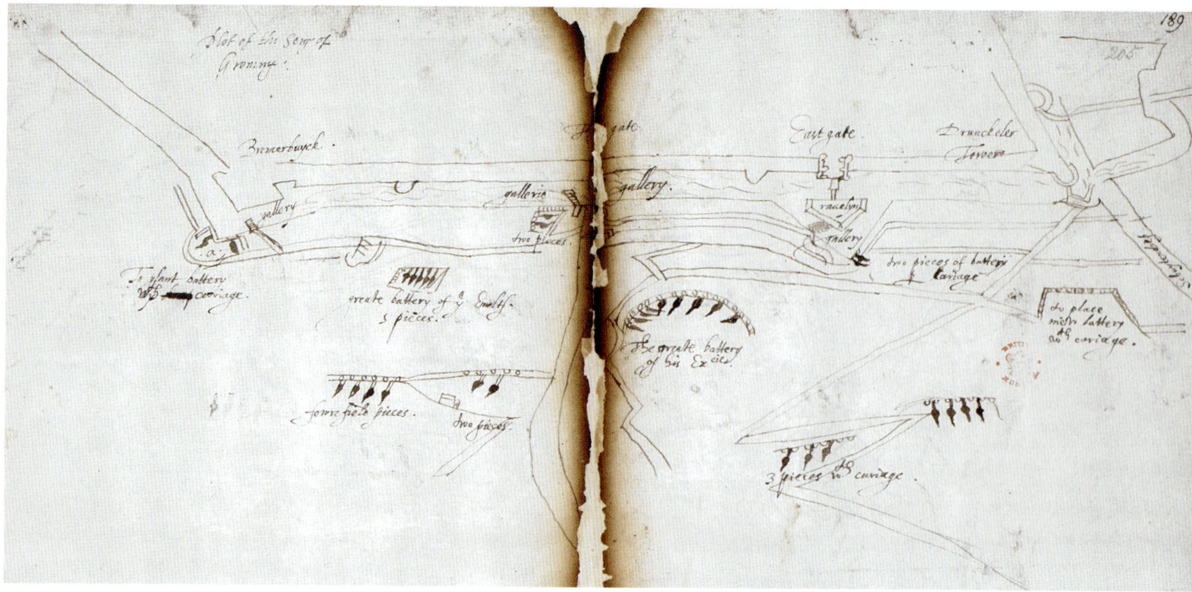

Figure 3.6a. (*top*) Sketch plan by Sir Thomas Bodley showing the siege of Groningen. BL Cotton MS Galba D.x.ff. 204v–205. © The British Library Board.

Figure 3.6b. (*bottom*) Robert Adams, proposal to relieve the Siege of Blaye in France by Catholic forces, 1592–93 (detail). BL Cotton MS Augustus I.ii.80. © The British Library Board.

immense detail expected, including the signs to be used for woods, hills, rocks, rivers, shelves in rivers, channels in rivers, and rocks in rivers both above and below the water, with instructions on how measurements in fathoms and in feet were to be rendered. The final, presentation version of these maps, however, would have been supplemented with ethnographical, zoological, and botanical illustrations in medieval, encyclopedic style (see fig. 3.1)—presentation maps were still regarded as being as much encyclopedic as purely geographical—to indicate the location of such phenomena (depicted in more detail in separate drawings) but also to make the overall image more appealing.

The first map in White's portfolio contains coastal profiles of the islands of Dominica and Santa Cruz (St. Croix) (fig. 3.8b). Though these are elegantly drafted, coastal views were utilitarian in purpose. The scale bar suggests, possibly incorrectly, that each profile covers about thirty nautical miles (though at the time the definition of the length of the mile varied from ours). Similar though much more elaborate printed examples are to be seen in Lucas Janszoon Waghenaer's contemporaneous and very influential nautical atlas, the *Spieghel der Zeevaerdt* (Leiden, 1584), which was translated into English by

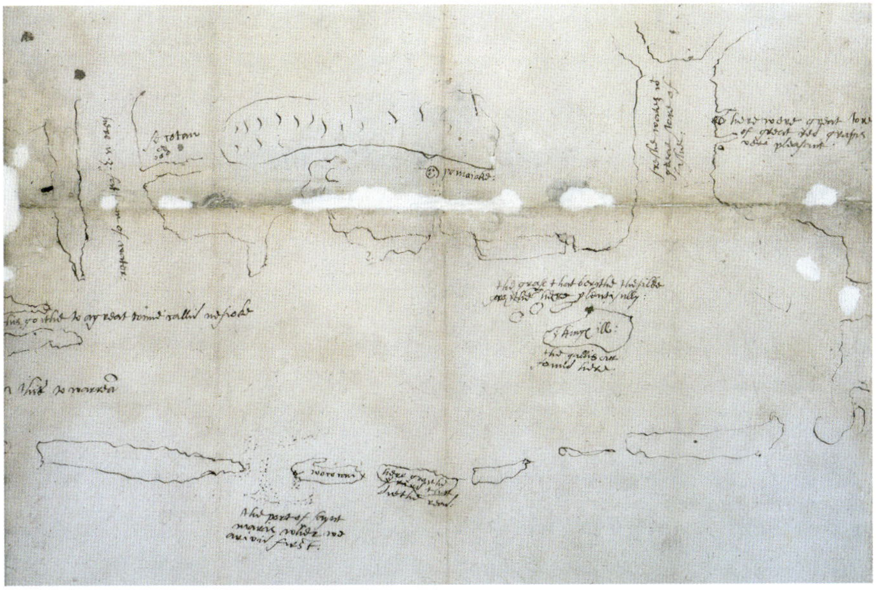

Figure 3.7. Sketch map of Roanoke Island and Albemarle Sound, ascribed to Ralph Lane, 1585. PRO/MPG1/584. © The National Archives, UK.

Anthony Ashley, the clerk to Queen Elizabeth's Privy Council, as *The Mariners' Mirrour* in 1588 (fig. 3.8a).

Next come fortification plans, though these are not simply plans. Like virtually all of White's maps in the British Museum set, they contain strong figurative and narrative elements, doubtless to meet the tenor of his instructions. At the stopping place in Puerto Rico, White drew the encampment created while Lane's men waited for the arrival of other ships from the squadron that had got dispersed at sea on their way from England (fig. 3.9b). It is technically a very sophisticated plan, with a scale bar at the bottom right. The fortifications and Lane's quarters at the top and those of the expedition commander, Sir Richard Grenville, at the bottom are shown in plan rather than in elevation or in bird's-eye perspective. Such ichnographic mapping demonstrated that White was in the cartographic vanguard. The plan is also highly decorative, showing men and ships and also the wildlife in the lake at the top right. In another drawing, White depicted the ambitious entrenchments, proudly called a fort, that the English erected nearby to protect themselves and their salt from the Spaniards (fig. 3.9a). Inside them we see two great mounds guarded by Lane and his men, who are shown busily taking the salt to their ship's boats.

White's instructions carry over to his watercolor of Secoton (see fig. 8.3). Though this may not immediately strike modern viewers as a map, bird's-eye views were artificial constructs and were classed with maps by White's contemporaries. They were also enormously popular, as demonstrated by the runaway success of *Civitates Orbis Terrarum*, a series of thick volumes of town maps and views, edited by Georg Braun and Franz Hogenberg in Cologne, from 1572. The view contains vignettes of Native American life copied from White's drawings but subordinated here, again in medieval style, to the overall design.

But what anyone will immediately recognize as a map is White's manuscript map of North America. This belongs to the third category. Geographic and even political accuracy are subordinated to propaganda, even more blatantly than the maps and ethnographical and botanical plates copied from lost originals by John White that accompany the *Briefe and true report of the new found land of Virginia*, published by Theodor de Bry in Frankfurt in 1590 (see fig. 2.14). The map does not have a scale bar, but there is a scale of latitude at the right, and at the lower left, the map depicts the hazards of Caribbean navigation.

Teylandt van Wicht twe mijlen van v. daer voorbij Zeijlende.
Tlandt van Beuchier met de Seuē clifen.
Tlandt van Fierlej alßmen daer voorbij zeijlenn.
ANGLIÆ PARS
Die Canael tusschen Engelandt en Vranckryck.
CANALIS INTER ANGLIAM ET FRANCIAM.
Beschrijvanghe der Zee Custen van Engelandt tusschen Wicht ende Doueren, met die princi pale hauenen ende gedaenten des selue Landts.

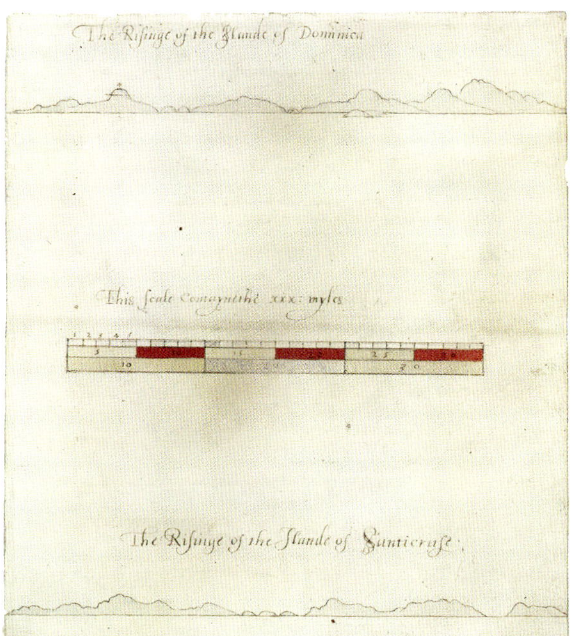
The Risinge of the Ilande of Dominica
This scale Contayneth xxx: myles
The Risinge of the Ilande of Santicruse

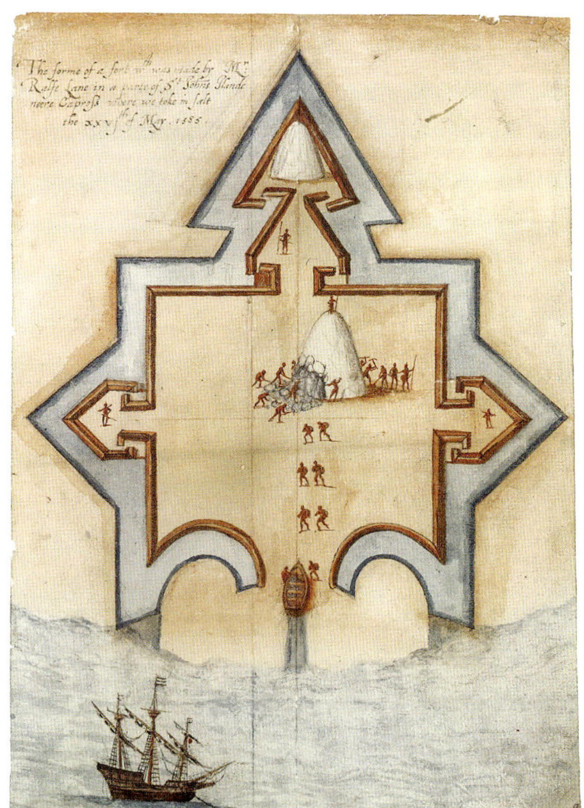
The forme of a fort wch was made by Mr Ralfe Lane in a parte of St Johns Ilande neere Capross where we toke in salt the xxvjth of May 1585

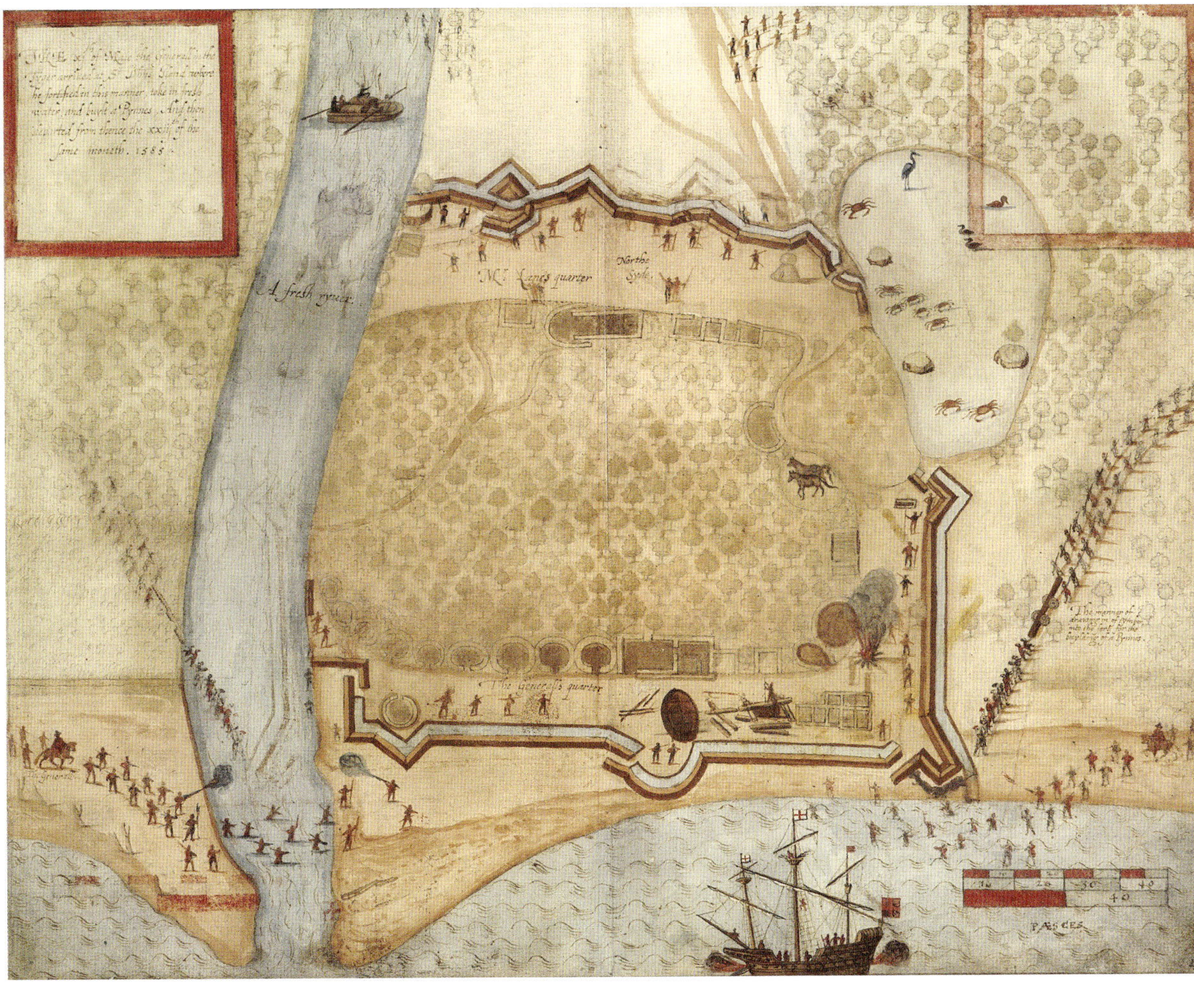

If the eastward drift of the North American coastline seems strange and wrong to modern eyes, this is due to the inability of map- and chart makers of the time to fix longitude accurately on land or at sea. This map has an agenda, however, that goes beyond geography. It focuses in an exaggerated way on the Virginia colony. In addition to the fantasy sea creatures that were becoming familiar on Flemish printed maps of the time, it again includes miniaturized versions of White's larger drawings—this time zoological—for instance, the flying fish.

When one places the great map of North America in a wider context, one sees that it has parallels with other contemporary and earlier maps. Just as it depicts the course of Lane's fleet on its way to Roanoke through a series of depictions of ships in the seas off the coasts of the

Figure 3.8a. (*opposite, top*)The coast of Sussex from Lucas Janszoon Waghenaer, *Spieghel der Zeevaerdt*, Leiden, 1584. Courtesy of Daniel Crouch Rare Books.

Figure 3.8b. (*opposite, bottom left*) John White, *Coastal Profiles of Dominica and Santa Cruz*, ca. 1585. British Museum, Dept. of Prints and Drawings, 1906,0509.1.36. © The Trustees of the British Museum.

Figure 3.9a. (*opposite, bottom right*) John White, *Plan of an Entrenchment near Cape Rojo, Puerto Rico*, ca. 1585. British Museum, Dept. of Prints and Drawings, 1906,0509.1.5. © The Trustees of the British Museum.

Figure 3.9b. (*above*) John White, *Plan of a Fortified Encampment at Mosquetal, Puerto Rico*, ca. 1585. British Museum, Dept. of Prints and Drawings, 1906,0509.1.4. © The Trustees of the British Museum.

NORTHE
SOVTHE
WEST
EAST
E R
SCOT
LANDE
LONDON
HOLLAND
FLANDERS
NORMANDIE

CIRCVLVSARTICVS
Terra agricule
Mare ibernicū
Mare terre noue
Mare oceanum:~
Insule aroreas
Mare hispanie
Mare galicū
Terra de florida
Oceanus occiduus
Insule fortunate
Mare antiliarum:~
TROPICVSCANCRI
ORIENS

Figure 3.10. (*opposite, top*) Augustine Ryther after Robert Adams, chart showing the track of the Armada, from Petruccio Ubaldini, *Expeditionis Hispaniorum in Angliam vero description*, 1590. Courtesy of Daniel Crouch Rare Books.

Figure 3.11. (*opposite, bottom*) Appropriation through heraldry: Diogo Homem, Chart of North Atlantic from *The Queen Mary Atlas*, 1555–59. BL Add. MS 5415 A, ff. 19v–20. © The British Library Board.

Figure 3.12. (*above*) Theodor de Bry after John White, *A Map of That Part of America Now Called "Virginia,"* 1590. Courtesy of Daniel Crouch Rare Books.

Caribbean Islands and North America, so when Robert Adams came to commemorate the defeat of the Spanish Armada on a map a few years later, he also showed the route of the Spanish fleet around a map of Great Britain and Ireland in the same way—albeit making the route clearer by way of a line (fig. 3.10). And despite the growing popularity of scientific precision, there was still mileage in the medieval assumption that what was important should occupy more space on a map than the unimportant even if the latter was larger in physical size. Thus, for political, commemorative, and propaganda purposes, on his map of North America, White enormously exaggerated the size of the Virginia colony, which is shown as extending deep into North America and down to Florida.

When it came to depicting pride of ownership, the rather rash and presumptuous display of Raleigh's coat of arms on White's map brings to mind—as no doubt intended—the display of the royal coats of arms of Spain and Portugal on contemporary maps of regions beyond Europe (fig. 3.11). What is most striking is the size of Raleigh's arms (see fig. 2.14). They dominate the continent where one might, at the least, have expected them to be coupled with those of Queen Elizabeth. This is surely the strongest indication that this map and the accompanying drawings were intended for Sir Walter personally. The situation was redressed in the map of Virginia published by de Bry in 1590, where the royal arms take precedence (fig. 3.12).

The Map *La Virginea Pars*

Let us turn to White's manuscript map showing the Virginia colony alone, *La Virginea Pars*, the "Part of [America Called] Virginia" (fig. 2.2). Like de Bry's printed map, also called *La Virginia Pars*, it has ships, coastal outlines, and coats of arms, but it shares little else. Indeed, if we compare the two maps, aligning both in the same direction, further differences become clear. The printed map extends much farther to the west—as almost certainly the manuscript map did before losing its left half, which compelled the letters of "Virginea Pars" to be added in the awkward way they are. But more significant is the greater level of information about the course of the rivers on the printed map. This strongly suggests that de Bry copied a later manuscript map, drawn perhaps in late 1586 or 1587. The printed map also shows other inland features that would have been required in White's instructions, such as woodland and hills as well as the miniaturized depictions of the Native peoples taken from large watercolors. All these elements are missing from the manuscript map.

On close examination it is evident that the manuscript map *La Virginea Pars* is very different from White's other surviving maps. The first thing to note is its relative austerity, despite its elegant execution. The often-remarked accuracy, demonstrated when it is compared to a remote sensing image of the same area, would have been valuable

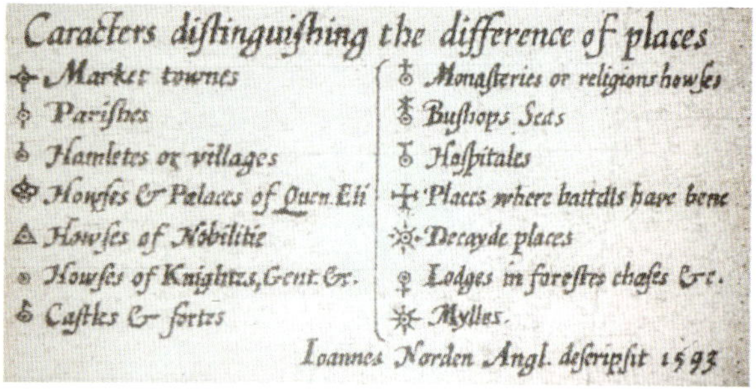

Figure 3.13a. (*top*) Key to signs on John Norden, *Myddlesex*, 1593. Courtesy of Daniel Crouch Rare Books.

Figure 3.13b. (*middle*) Extract showing the coasts near Lewes from *A Survey made by Sir Thomas Palmere Knight and Mister Waltar Couerte esquire Deputie Lieutenants of her Majesties Countie of Sussex of all the places of descente alongste the sea coaste of the said Shire*, 1587. BL Add. MS 57494. © The British Library Board.

Figure 3.13c. (*bottom*) Detail from a manuscript map of Ulster attributed to John Norden, 1610. BL Cotton MS Augustus I.i.44. © The British Library Board.

Figure 3.14. (*opposite*) Details from the anonymous "Long View" of the southwestern coasts of England, 1539–40, showing the annotations "made," "not made," and "half made," relating to proposed new coastal fortifications. BL Cotton MS Augustus I.i.35, 36, 38, 39. © The British Library Board.

for planning as well as scholarly and propaganda purposes. The patches are hardly what one would expect in a presentation piece. Moreover, the interior is empty and lacking in almost all the detailed information that had been required in Bavin's instructions. Instead, one is left with simple coastal outlines adorned perhaps with the odd ship. Settlements are indicated by a utilitarian circle, which recalls the sort of unadorned signs for minor places to be found in European maps of the time, such as John Norden's map of the county of Middlesex of 1593 (fig. 3.13a). Even the apparently decorative features are not what they seem. The ships convey information about where Lane's ships landed, and in this context the canoes are particularly interesting. Far from being ornaments, their positions are intended to indicate shallow waters unsuitable for larger ships. So, taken together, the ships and canoes convey important navigational information.

Now let us look at the coloring of the Outer Banks on the map. I would cautiously suggest that the selection of colors may not be primarily decorative but may denote perceptions of ownership of land by the various Native inhabitants and perhaps indicate their rumored attitudes toward the colonists: similar conventions are found in contemporary English and continental maps. Indeed, looking at the map as a whole, what is most striking is its overall resemblance to a series of equally elegant and precise manuscript maps of 1587 showing the coasts of the English county of Sussex. They were intended as an aid to preparing defenses against a Spanish attack, a threat that seemed as great as that to Raleigh's Virginia, and like *La Virginea Pars*, these maps located the homes of possible traitors: Indians on White's map, the Catholic Mr. Gage of Firle Place in Sussex on Palmer and Covert's map of the Sussex coast (fig. 3.13b).

And there are the famous patches. The patches are different in nature from the flaps that are to be found on several Tudor fortification

plans and maps of battles, where they depict how the finished fort would look or what the besieged town looked like after a siege. In the case of *La Virginea Pars*, the patches seem to have been economy measures to avoid the labor of redrawing the whole map. I know of no other examples, but such working maps are unlikely to have been preserved—unless there were particular reasons for keeping them—as in this case.

The lower patch has been shown to conceal a correction to the coastline. In itself that was not particularly surprising. It was a surprise, however, to discover that the upper patch concealed the outline of a four-bastioned fort (see fig. 2.7). This resembles the simple forts that were then being built by the English in its other, older colony, Ireland, and in the Netherlands, the former in a somewhat later plan of about 1610 attributed to John Norden (fig. 3.13c) and the latter in a sketch map by Sir Thomas Bodley of 1593. In all three cases, however, given the scale of the maps, the depictions of forts are probably conventionalized and should not without further investigation be regarded as representing the reality.

What was the original purpose of the map *La Virginea Pars*? I would suggest that it was—like the map of the Sussex coastlines prepared a year later—an elegantly executed planning document. Dating from 1539–40 and intended to defend England from attack by France and Spain, an equally elegant map was annotated to show the locations of possible new forts (fig. 3.14). Just as this earlier map was continuously being annotated to show forts that were "made" or "not made," or only "half made," so *La Virginea Pars* continued to be adapted. Not only were

Figure 3.15. Anon. (from Edward Wright), chart of the western approaches to England, after 1589. BL Cotton MS Augustus I.i.14. © The British Library Board.

coastlines improved, but the cartographer placed a patch over a fort, suggesting that he believed that it no longer existed or had not yet been built at all (it is a besetting sin of mapmakers to show what was only suggested as an actual building). And then renewed lines over the patch appeared as the proposal for a colonial presence there was reconsidered.

Why did a planning document end up with a set of watercolors and commemorative maps and plans intended for presentation in line with White's and Harriot's instructions? I would suggest that originally the set included an earlier version of the map of Virginia that was to be published by de Bry, but that perhaps as early as the 1590s this map had been destroyed or badly damaged. In the rush to replace it, *La Virginea Pars* was taken from Walter Raleigh's papers and substituted, even though it had been intended to serve a quite different purpose and despite the differences in detail between it and the damaged or destroyed map.

After all, such planning maps intended for the eyes of the high and mighty could be very pretty. That is also the case with related manuscript maps of the early 1590s by Harriot's associate Edward Wright for Secretary Burghley that were intended to help fend off a second Spanish Armada (fig. 3.15). And England's preoccupation with that very threat was the real reason for the final failure of the threat-doomed Roanoke colony.

chapter four

IMAGES AND ABSENCES

Interpreting John White's Maps

Eric Klingelhofer

The inquiry in 2012 by First Colony Foundation resulted in the discovery by the British Museum staff of a hidden symbol on John White's watercolor *La Virginea Pars* map, as Kim Sloan has related. The staff's subsequent multispectrum analysis of the map revealed hitherto unknown changes. Discussions with curator Kim Sloan and scientist Janet Ambers led, first, to my close examination of all four picture maps in the White portfolio in 2013 and, subsequently, to First Colony Foundation's sponsored spectrographic analysis of substances used to color details on those drawings, which the museum completed in 2014 (see frontispiece).

This second study answered questions specific to this map. The first analysis determined that White's palette included various reds and indigo for blue, but on Raleigh's coat of arms, there was smalt (a cobalt compound) for blue, plus now-blackened silver, and even orpiment (arsenic sulfide) for gold coloring. From the chemical elements of the coloring components, the second tests concluded that White had used a four-part color scheme over graphite pencil outlines, lightening or darkening each by water dilution. Red lead and red lake (aluminum compound) was used for dots marking Indian villages and for islands, diluted to a pink to color larger areas. A second type was based on the hematite in red ocher, commonly used since prehistory for ritual or honorific coloring of the skin. White applied it thinly to areas in the sea where shoals had been seen. A third type was a mixture of vermilion and red lead, which stands out in Raleigh's coat of arms. British Museum scientists observed that this was used elsewhere only on islands outlined in red, but without internal coloring. Aside from the blue coastal colorant, others appear to have been organic and could not have withstood the soaking at Sotheby's in 1865; a faint yellow tint survives on some of the larger islands and coastline. These scientific studies helped us understand not only how the map was produced and where it was altered but also what information could be drawn from the small details within all four picture maps left by John White.

White labeled his portfolio *The pictures of sondry things collected and counterfeited according to the truth in the voyage made by Sir Walter Raleigh knight, for the discovery of La Virginea.1585* (see fig. 2.15). Sketches for these watercolors would have been made on the expedition to North Carolina via the West Indies, led by Sir Richard Grenville on behalf of his cousin Raleigh. Less attention has been paid to the picture maps than to White's series of New World anthropological and biological drawings. His pictures of plants, animals, and Native peoples are rightly heralded as evidence of the first importance. They supplement the written study of the New World by Thomas Harriot, the Renaissance scientist in Sir Walter's employ. While Harriot remained with the Virginia colony until the following summer, it is now recognized that John White set sail from "Virginia" with Grenville on August 25, 1585.

White was not a member of the Roanoke Island military colony that was tasked with exploring the region, so the four picture maps would have served a different purpose. Important expeditions by other leaders received the same kind of visual record, such as Baptista Boazio's picture maps of Sir Francis Drake's raid on Spanish towns in the Caribbean in 1585–86. Boazio traveled in the entourage of Christopher Carlisle, lieutenant general of the expedition's field army. Carlisle was the stepson of Sir Francis Walsingham, whose intelligence service would have wanted maps of strategic Spanish cities. The *Notes geven to Master Candishe* of recommendations for the voyage of 1585 call for a "good geographer to make discription of the lands discouerd, and with hym an exilent paynter." Similarly, the realistic drawing in White's portfolio of Inuit fighting English in a ship's boat suggests that Sir Martin Frobisher, too, may have had an artist on his voyages in search of a Northwest Passage. In 1583, the wealthy cloth merchant and lord mayor of London Sir Edward Osborne sent to India a group that included the painter James Story, who seems to have remained in Goa.

The *Virgenia Pars* Voyage Map

Key elements of this map of the southeast coast of North America are the compass rose, Raleigh's arms, and the latitude scale. Filled with ships and marine wildlife, *La Virgenia Pars* (see fig. 2.14) omits the earlier portion of the voyage to depict Grenville's sailing along the American coast until coming to anchor off the Roanoke inlets. Presumably requested by Raleigh, the map has a centrally placed latitudinal scale that sets English Virginia, French and Spanish Florida, the Bahamas, and even Norumbega (New England–Nova Scotia) in their correct geographic positions and at the same scale. This page has been heavily trimmed—cutting through names on Florida's west coast and both the names Norumbega and La Bermuda—so it may well once have shown the full coastline between Cape Henry, Virginia, and Newfoundland, the claim to which Raleigh may have aspired. From what remains, Harriot's geography improved greatly over that in the contemporary *Drake Voyage* by Boazio and is probably closer to that on the globe that Emery Molyneux made in 1592. Molineux had also participated in a Drake voyage, the circumnavigation of 1577. Close inspection of the White map confirms what may be an idiosyncrasy on his part or perhaps a convention of miniaturists: the period after a word is not actually a round dot but a tiny cross-hatch or asterisk.

Kim Sloan has pointed out that the latitude shown for Roanoke is inaccurate by a full degree, suggesting that it could have been deliberate to mislead competitors and Spanish spies. But White does show the site of the French former colony of Charlesfort in Florida, and his coloring seems to make Port Royal in South Carolina the border between the English colony and that of French claims. At the same time, he ignores St. Augustine, which Drake attacked and burned on his way to Roanoke in 1586. The English may have assumed that its thorough destruction led the Spanish to abandon it.

The Verrazano Sea (*Mare de Verrazana*) was thought to be an arm of the Pacific, and it appears so on the map from 1582 published by Michael Lok (or Locke), a financer of voyages in search of the Northwest Passage (fig. 4.1). What Giovanni da Verrazzano saw in 1524 were actually the North Carolina Sounds. Here, the "sea" has been moved to the end of a river that runs down to Port Royal,

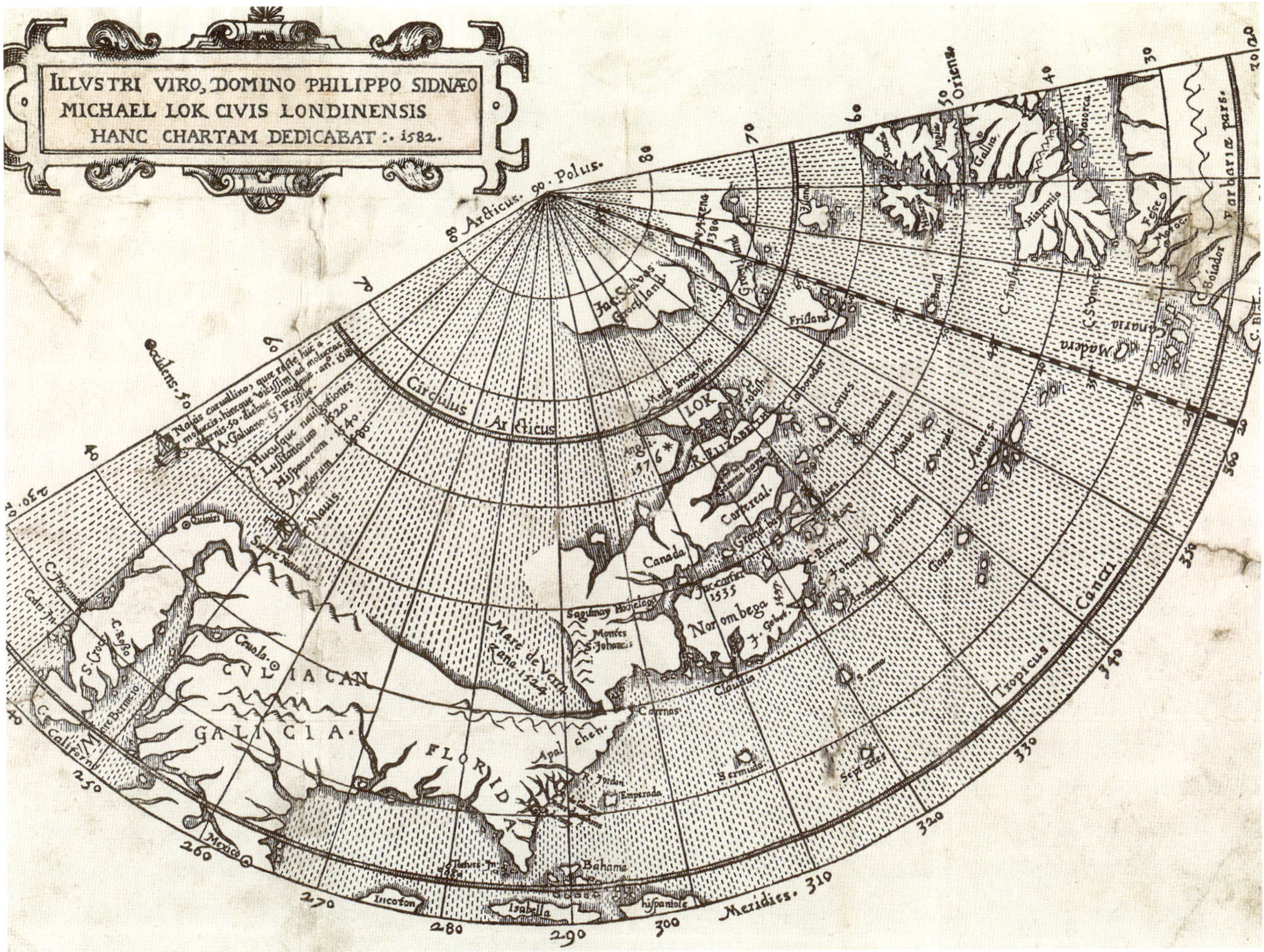

Figure 4.1. *Illustri Viro . . .* , map of North America, Michael Lok and Thomas Woodcock, London, 1582. Osher Map Library map/316.0001, University of Southern Maine.

South Carolina. Its presence is probably due to Indian accounts of an inland sea. Because White leaves it uncolored, along with two better-defined lakes in Florida, Harriot may have considered it a freshwater body.

The large, brightly colored arms of Raleigh—with no royal arms depicted here—suggests to Peter Barber that this watercolor was made for Sir Walter personally and may have been intended for use or display in his London home, Durham House. Differences between this *Virgenia Pars* Voyage Map and the *Virginea Pars* Exploration Map—overall brighter colors and prominent sea beasts—support this idea. It was not used by de Bry and may not have been given to him. The quality of the image reveals White's skill in drawing elaborate heraldry, no doubt part of his work as a painter of court pageantry.

Figure 4.2. Detail of Albemarle Sound section of *La Virginea Pars* map (see fig. 2.2), with insert of pinnace underdrawing revealed by infrared reflectogram. Photo by Kim Sloan.

The map shows six ships, but these may well be the same three-masted vessel with the St. George red cross flag on its mainmast in both transatlantic voyages, the same again shown twice coasting north from Florida, and then shown again twice anchored off the Carolina Banks. The ship would be Grenville's admiral (flagship), H.M.S. *Tiger*, on which White sailed. It displays a rear lantern and four gold-colored guns below-decks. An erased flag (in reversed direction) once flew from the aft mast. The afterdeck and fore-deck have rounded roofs; they are colored not white or cream, like the sails, but a brown shade that is lighter than the rest of the ship. Most likely this represents hooped tenting of waxed canvas, made of hemp or coarse linen. Such waxing is recorded as early as the 1300s, in contrast to oil-skin, which is first recorded around 1800.

Details of the North Carolina coast and Virginia south of the Chesapeake follow those of the *Virginea Pars* map, discussed next, and we find duplicate errors: two village red-dot symbols at Dasemunkepeuc (on the mainland opposite Roanoke Island) and no village symbol on the west shore of the Albemarle Sound, where White applied a patch onto the Exploration Map that covered the symbol for Mettaquem village. Red dots are given to all the other villages in the Albemarle, and most names are present. Thus, the *Virgenia Pars* Voyage Map must have been drawn after the *Virginea Pars* Exploration Map was completed and then altered. The Voyage Map also has colored islands, but whether intentional or due to its small scale, only the red is visible to the eye.

The *Virginea Pars* Exploration Map

The Exploration Map (see fig. 2.6) differs most significantly from the Voyage Map in its decorative elements: more subdued colors, absence of sea creatures, more modest arms of Sir Walter Raleigh with larger royal arms given prominence, dominant compass, and no latitude scale. This map could be shown at Elizabeth's court and to the Privy Council.

Similar details in the two maps suggest that the Exploration Map was drawn first and that the Voyage Map copied it at a considerably smaller scale. White had the trait of placing a period after each place-name, but the colorist here mistook it for a second village symbol for Dasemunkepeuc, on the mainland opposite Roanoke, and colored it red. As noted above, the Voyage Map also has two red dots there (fig. 4.2).

The Exploration Map also marks the *Roanoac* village as a red dot between the island's Northwest Point and a northeastern point, at the approximate location of Fort Raleigh National Historic Site. The northeastern point is flanked to the south by an exaggerated cove (or Elizabethan "creek"), both since lost to erosion. The village location is duplicated on the Voyage Map. South of the cove is a faint circle, possibly erased, which the colorist did not use for the *Roanoac* village, but that location is where de Bry placed the village in his *Arrival of the Englishmen in Virginia* print (see fig. 1.1), which Kim Sloan believes was taken from an unknown drawing by White. The absence of Shallowbag Bay here is not unexpected because later colonial maps depict it as a stream passing through marshland.

The Exploration Map retains enough of the coloring for us to see that the islands and some mainland coasts were given different colors. Light red, orange, and green wash were used. Nearly all the mainland coast is edged with a dark blue, which is lacking only in the far south. The coastline from Croatamung island to the Chesapeake Bay was considered a potential island and was given a green wash. If not purely decorative, but in some way informative, as Peter Barber has suggested, the different colors may represent territories of allies to the English: the Roanokes and the Croatans. These lands are colored light red or pink, which Janet Ambers identified as made from madder, a common vegetable dye. In April 1586, Governor Lane established good relations with the Chowanoke tribe, whose lands are not colored here. It may be that the coloring represents the political situation in the late summer of 1585, when Grenville and White left for England. But it might also represent the lands that Raleigh recognized as belonging to the Christian prince Manteo of Croatoan, who was inaugurated as Lord of Roanoke and Dasemunkepeuc in August 1587.

Turning our attention to images depicted here, the most common must be the many Indians in canoes. Peter Barber suggests that they are not decorative but indicate areas where the water is too shallow for English boats, which is often the case in the Carolina Sounds. But the images, as small as they are, yield additional information about the subjects. All canoes have at least one standing figure, and no seated or kneeling figure is depicted paddling. Here, Carolina Algonquians stood to propel and steer dugout canoes, shown also in White's drawing of them fishing,

Figure 4.3. Algonquian dugout canoe propelled by standing boatsmen using long-handled paddles, not unlike Venetian gondoliers. John White, *Indians Fishing*, ca. 1585. British Museum, Dept. of Prints and Drawings, 1906,0509.1.6. © The Trustees of the British Museum.

employing long-handled paddles for that purpose (fig. 4.3). This provided them with fulcrum leverage not needed for the lighter birchbark canoes available in the north.

Another common image is the small, one-masted vessel that was used to explore the sounds. An image of this vessel had been drawn in graphite entering the southern of two inlets separated by a small island, but it was erased and replaced by a larger ship at anchor. The inlet and the island were noted in reports, and the southern inlet was initially named Port Fernando after the expedition's pilot, the Portuguese Simon Fernandes, from the Azores. The islands of the banks are provided names on the picture map, but not the inlets through them. Just inside the sound there is a flattened X-like mark in the same red-brown color used for canoes and ship hulls. It appears that part of the mark overlies a tiny, darker-colored islet inside the sound and was therefore drawn somewhat later. Unlike the reddish islets by White's "Sho" (for Shoal), written in Currituck Sound (Titepano) to the north, the X-mark may be a foreshortened canoe, which could also indicate shallow water near the passage to Roanoke (see fig. 4.2).

Ships, too, were altered as the picture map was made. Janet Ambers and British Museum conservators discovered though infrared reflectography that the southernmost ships, as painted in watercolor, do not fully conform to the graphite lines that sketched them. Another detail that was changed is the erased anchor rope on the ship nearest the scale. Because the vessel is under sail, it could not be anchored, so the artist corrected the error. A more dramatic change is seen in the small, one-masted exploration vessel sailing east from the far end of the Albemarle Sound (fig. 4.2). Again, infrared reflectography revealed graphite lines differing from the visible image. In this case, the original vessel was a smaller type that lacked a raised afterdeck, had one sail, but was also propelled by oars. This describes a pinnace and may well be the one built in Puerto Rico for exploring inland. Also surprising, the pinnace was heading west, not east. The decision to alter the type of vessel and its direction is not readily explained. It probably took place before the picture map was finished and may be related to the erasure of the single-masted vessel outside Port Fernando.

The same work-in-progress corrections occurred in the lower of the two small patches that have been attached to the map since the sixteenth century. Kim Sloan and Peter Barber have discussed the patches, and infrared imaging reveals that the southern patch, over part of the Pamlico Sound, covered geographic errors in graphite, and then watercolors were applied to the area. The patch also covered the graphite circle symbol for the town of Aquascagoc and most of the circle for Secotaoc. The colorist then placed red dots near those names but not directly on the original locations (see figs. 2.4 and 2.5).

The southern patch was added during assemblage of the picture map, but the northern patch, at the west end of the Albemarle Sound, was added after the map was finished because it lies over the watercolor. The northern patch covers an opening in the shoreline, the harbor of what is now Salmon Creek (see figs. 2.6 and 2.7). It also covers the red dot–circle of an Indian settlement on the north side of the harbor. De Bry's printed version of this map from 1590 identifies this as Mettaquem, one of the towns that Lane mentioned in his exploration of the Chowan River. It came under the authority of Menatonan, king of the Chowanokes, who soon allied with the English against Wingina and the Roanokes.

But covering the town of Mettaquem was incidental to the patch's real purpose: to hide the boldly colored blue-and-red fort symbol drawn at Salmon Creek. This was a standard representation of a Renaissance-style fort, with rectangular curtain walls, four angled bastions, and what looks like a corps de guard headquarters or barrack building in the center (fig. 4.4a). The patch not only hid the fort symbol but replaced it with another type (see fig. 2.6). Barely visible even under magnification, it had been drawn with what Janet Ambers of the British Museum considered possibly invisible ink. This new image was that of another common Renaissance symbol, the fortified city (fig. 4.4b). Always designed with regularity and symmetry, but of various shapes, such city plans typically had external defenses and a central citadel.

The sequence of symbols here, first Mettaquem village, then fort, then town, informs us of the changing identities that Raleigh's men gave to this locality. It is logical that the town replaced the fort when the civilian colony was established in lieu of a relieved military colony. And perhaps Raleigh kept a secret town image ready to show how precisely he knew the colony's location if his charter were to be challenged on the grounds that none of his settlers occupied the land he had been granted.

I cannot say that the two images, above and below the patch, depict specific entities that Raleigh wanted to be established in America. More likely, they are symbols of his intentions. Grenville's exploration of Pamlico Sound found little of value, but Lane's expeditions beyond the Albemarle Sound (then apparently also known as Roanoke) seemed to confirm the expedition of 1584's tales of distant treasure. The Chowan River, controlled by the allied Chowanoke king, could be followed northeast toward the James River and its island of pearls, and the Moratuc River (now Roanoke) could lead northwest to deposits of copper and silver.

The patch reflects Raleigh's changing ideas on how this wealth was to be obtained. First, a fortified base serving as the gateway for travel and trade up the two rivers to Ralph Lane's twin goals. Here, the colony would be male and military to ensure a commercial exploitation of resources, similar to the Portuguese Empire's

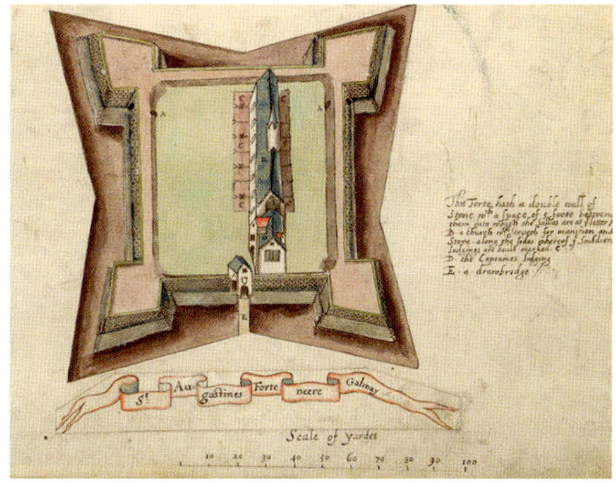

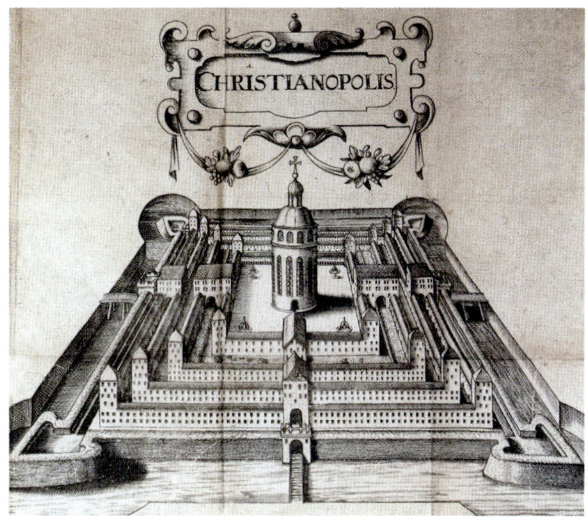

Figure 4.4a. (*top*) St. Augustine's Fort, Donegal, Ireland, 1603. *Architecture of Galway* and *Lost Buildings of Ireland*, www.archiseek.com/2014/1603-st-augustines-fort-galway.

Figure 4.4b. (*bottom*) Johann Andreae, image of the utopian city *Christianopolis*, Strasburg: Lazarus Zetzner, 1619.

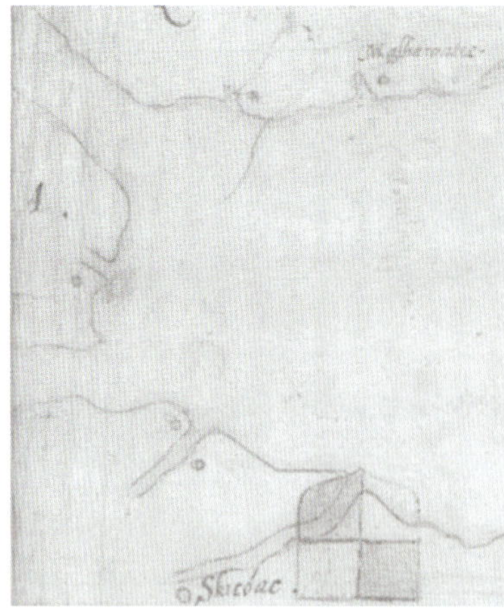

Figure 4.5. (*left*) Detail of *La Virginea Pars* map (see fig. 2.2 for full map), showing mouth of James River.

Figure 4.6. (*middle*) Infrared image of figure 4.5. Photo by Kim Sloan.

Figure 4.7. (*right*) Detail of same area in Theodor de Bry's *Virginia* map (see fig. 3.12). North to right. Library of Congress.

trading "castles" in the Old World and Brazil. This may well have been what his brother, Sir Humphrey Gilbert, had in mind for Newfoundland and Norumbega. But support for this model soon faded, perhaps under pressure from the realities of an open war with Spain. The Virginia colony, as first planned, failed to provide the safe harbor for privateers to pluck quick profits off Spanish galleons. The hoped-for treasures of pearls and silver, and even the less valuable copper, were unproven hopes. Raleigh turned to another model to maintain his possession of Virginia by meeting requirements detailed in his grant from the Crown. While trade with the Native Americans for furs, medicinal plants, silver, and pearls would continue, a civilian colony would establish a town, the "Cittie of Ralegh," which could avoid conflict with the Indians by creating its own agriculture base. The settlement would be self-sufficient, with farms of fields and pastures on the higher, richer soils that begin at the head of the Albemarle Sound. As reported by John White himself, those settlers planned to take their families "50 mile into the Maine" to what the map informs us was Mettaquem village and a safe harbor near the mouth of the Chowan, the expected gateway to North America.

Chesapeake

It is in the Chesapeake that we find our last area of significant alterations (fig. 4.5). Quickly noticeable is the small triangular island in Hampton Roads waters, a later addition because its simple outline was inked over the light blue wash of the water, while the island itself was never recolored. It does not appear in the infrared image (fig. 4.6). The British Museum determined that its inked lines were of iron gall, which seems not to have been used by White. David Beers Quinn thought that this island was the one that Lane had heard to be the seat of a powerful king and the source of pearls.

On the central peninsula of the adjacent mainland, the Native town of Kecoughtan is marked as a red dot or circle west of the small Hampton River. Changes were made here at the same time as the island was added. Infrared imaging reveals no evidence of White's graphite beyond the mouth of the river at *Kecoughtan*, which iron-gall ink altered without watercolor to be longer and more prominent. The same ink was used over the blue shoreline to narrow the mouth of the river, a presumed correction. Feathered lines outside the river's mouth could indicate shoals, but they are

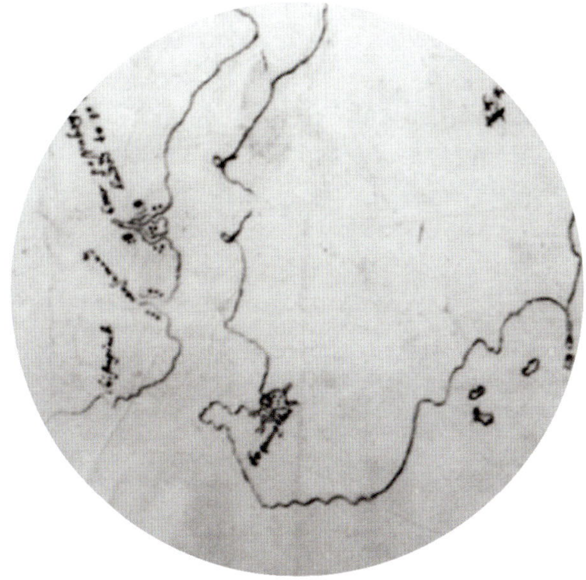

Figure 4.8. Detail of Smith-Zuniga map (see fig. 10.3), showing mouth of James River and Kecoughtan.

not the light brown wash used for all other shoals on the map. Like the river's mouth, it may have been a geographic correction for which watercolor was unavailable. A plausible explanation, which lacks definitive evidence, is that it marked the erasure of the island that was then repositioned offshore.

First appearing as an addition to White's manuscript map, this island was firmly established in the Hampton Roads channel on de Bry's map of "Virginia" from 1590 (fig. 4.7). Following Lane's report of the island of pearls and his advice to send ships to the Chesapeake to reach the Chowan for metals, the lower James River had increased importance. The crudeness of the drawings and the use of iron gall suggest that White was not responsible for the additions. They must have been drawn by someone else close to Raleigh, possibly Thomas Harriot himself.

The founding of Jamestown in 1607 presents us with more information. In February 1609, Thomas Harriot was still viewed as an authority on the geography of the area when he spoke to a meeting of the Virginia Company about the location of silver mines reported to him in the 1580s. All maps of early Jacobean settlements were kept secret and have not survived, but the Smith-Zuniga Map of 1611 is a spy's copy of John Smith's map of both Virginia and Carolina (see fig. 4.8). It shows Kecoughtan town on the north side of the entrance to the James River, at Hampton Roads. To the right of the town is the small bay of Hampton River, and to the right of that is a small island, linked to the mainland by a narrow strand that may have been regularly submerged.

David Quinn noted that soon after this, Richard Strachey, the secretary of the colony, reported: "There is extant an old plott, which his Lordship hath shewed me, wherein by a Portugall our seat is layd out, and in the same 2 silver Mynes pricked out." The "Seat" should refer to the colonized portion of the Chesapeake region, not just Jamestown. It is probable that the Anglo-Portuguese pilot Simon Fernandes had some knowledge of the area, likely from a Spanish sea chart of the route to the destroyed Jesuit mission of Jacan in the Bay of Santa Maria. The new governor, Lord De La Warr, could have been given this "old plot" by Raleigh himself, then confined to the Tower of London, or by his agent Thomas Harriot, or even by Richard Hakluyt, who had published the voyages. Maps contain an extraordinary amount of information about their subject, their use, and even their creation. It is just so with John White's and Thomas Harriot's mutual masterpiece, *La Virginea Pars*, a map fit for a queen.

part three

SITE X

Figure pt.3.1. Theodor de Bry map of *Virginia*. In "Wunderbarliche, doch warhafftige Erklärung, von der Gelegenheit vnd Sitten der Wilden in Virginia . . . ," *America*, pt. 1, Frankfurt: Theodor de Bry, 1590. North Carolina Collection, Wilson Library, University of North Carolina at Chapel Hill.

The British Museum's discovery in 2012 of a hidden fort symbol on John White's manuscript map of *La Virginea Pars* Virginia of 1585 raised questions about the fort's location at the head of the Albemarle Sound and its potential as a clue to the mystery of Sir Walter Raleigh's Lost Colonists. To answer these questions, First Colony Foundation researchers had three objectives: obtain documentary and cartographic information on the Salmon Creek area of Bertie County, determine the spatial extent of the early colonial presence on Salmon Creek, and collect additional data from Site BR146, the provenance of potential sixteenth-century ceramics.

Some members of our team were already familiar with Salmon Creek in Bertie County. In 2007, professional archaeologists Nick Luccketti and Gordon Watts had been called to examine the thousand-acre Bal Gra Plantation, in advance of a proposed residential and boating development that later failed to materialize. At Bal Gra, they surveyed and tested a large prehistoric settlement site on the north side of Salmon Creek's wide mouth. Prehistorian Clay Swindell judged it to have been occupied into the last precolonial years of the Late Woodland Period. Because a few English potsherds of potential sixteenth-century date were discovered in location 31BR246 peripheral to the main area of Indian habitation, identifying the main site was important to understanding the peripheral one (fig. pt.3.1).

We soon determined that the Native town site on Salmon Creek was that known to the Elizabethans as Mettaquem. As discussed in the previous chapter, John White's *La Virginea Pars* map of 1585 was altered soon after he drew it. The fort symbol was covered with a patch that also masked the red dot representing the Indian town. Yet other copies of the map retained the original identification, but without the fort, and one of these must have been the basis of the map published by Theodor de Bry in 1590. Governor Ralph Lane did mention the village in his report of 1586, apparently listing it among the towns of Weapemeoc, a territory ruled by the king Okisco, though Lane does not say that he visited it. Significantly, de Bry showed only one well-enclosed harbor on the Albemarle Sound and its tributaries: Salmon Creek. All the other openings on the sound are watercourses or open-ended, as if not fully explored. English colonial authorities, then, showed an interest in the Salmon Creek harbor, even if the creek itself was unsuitable for seafaring vessels. It could be argued, however, that even though the Native town symbol must refer to Mettaquem, the location was of little importance because it wasn't given a name on the *Virginea Pars* map. The inked name could have been erased, while the heavily colored fort needed to be covered over. But several other such town symbols were not named: two faint ones on Core Sound north of Cape Lookout and four brighter symbols on Chesapeake shores. To get to the truth of the matter, it was time to leave the map room and return to the field.

In the sections that follow, I review the various scientific techniques we used to determine on the ground what the British Museum map symbols may have indicated. Then, archaeologist Nick Luccketti presents the evidence we unearthed at Site X and how it must relate to the Lost Colonists. Later, FCF prehistorian Clay Swindell describes the Carolina Algonquians and what we have learned about the town of Mettaquem.

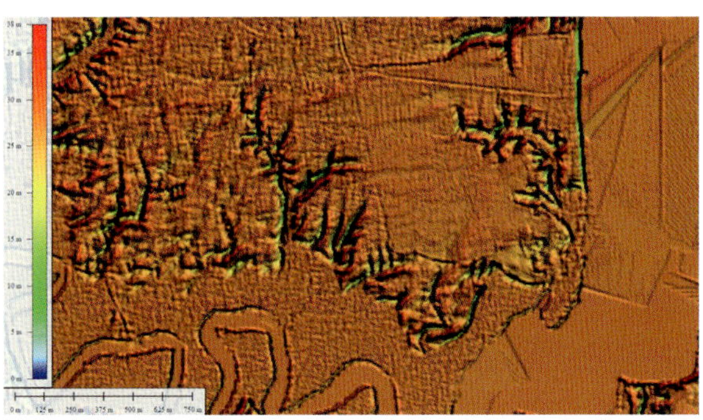

Figure 5.1. (*top*) Infrared image of Bertie County area on lower Salmon Creek. Albemarle Sound to right. First Colony Foundation.

Figure 5.2. (*bottom*) Lidar image of ground surface on north side of Salmon Creek harbor. First Colony Foundation.

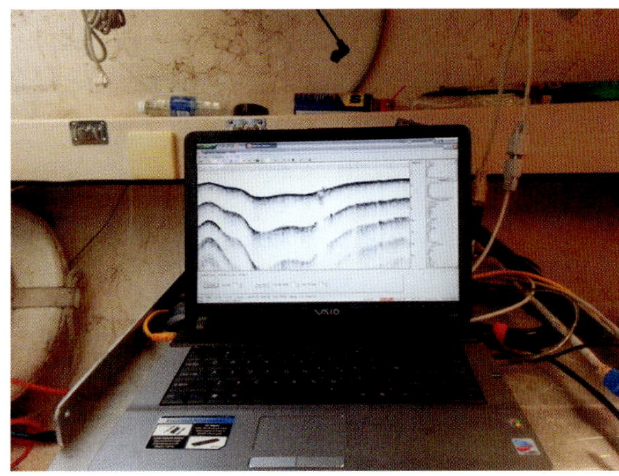

Figure 5.3. Screen of Sidescan Sonar image of large, submerged anomaly near Site X. Photo by Gordon Watts

chapter five

SCIENCE IN THE SEARCH

Eric Klingelhofer

With the possibility that an Elizabethan settlement had been proposed for present-day Bertie County, the First Colony Foundation team undertook a series of steps in 2012–13 to determine its likely location. Historical maps indicate locations of later colonial and US farmsteads around Salmon Creek, and team members had already researched that material in 2007 for their report on the archaeological survey. We also looked for evidence in the North Carolina state archaeological collections from the vicinity, but no possible Elizabethan artifacts were located in any of the inventoried material, which reinforced the significance of the artifacts recovered at Mettaquem.

We returned to the field for a surface survey at the Lawrence Farm on the next plateau upstream, but that yielded a few modern finds—nothing older. I obtained a National Geographic–Waitt Exploration Grant for scientific research to locate possible sites and brought in physicist Malcolm LeCompte of Elizabeth City State University to lead satellite-based remote sensing (fig. 5.1). Multispectrum imaging revealed the locations of former farmhouses and the circular geological formations called Carolina Bays, but nothing like a Renaissance fort. Lidar (light detection and ranging) imaging of ground surface showed ravines, fields, and farm roads but no topographic features resembling a settlement like Jamestown or Plymouth (fig. 5.2). Meanwhile, Gordon Watts carried out an underwater remote-sensing survey of Salmon Creek; its numerous readings indicated several submerged wooden vessels, all small craft except for one larger target near the creek's mouth (fig. 5.3).

We augmented these necessary if ultimately unproductive projects by two direct efforts to collect data at 31BR246, the small area of potential sixteenth-century finds adjacent to Mettaquem, by test excavation yielding features and artifacts, and finally by surface-based remote sensing. The excavation took place in November 2012, under the overall direction of archaeologist Nick Luccketti, who named the location "Site X" because there was no explanation for the handful of small, broken Elizabethan-type potsherds turning up in a low strip of land between two cypress swamps in Bertie County (fig. 5.4). We just hoped that they had not been dumped there in modern land-filling operations to create a beach on the Salmon Creek frontage and an unpaved access road to it. Details of the excavation are discussed in the following section, but importantly, the excavation in 2012 corroborated the recovery in 2007 of artifacts usually associated with

Figure 5.4. Vegetation false imaging of land surface around Site X. First Colony Foundation.

Figure 5.5. Ground-penetrating radar operated at Site X by physicist Malcolm LeCompte (*left*), assisted by FCF officer Alastair Macdonald (*right*). First Colony Foundation.

the Elizabethan period. It did appear, though, that later activities on the site obscured what structural evidence remained of an Elizabethan presence.

The second direct examination of Site X was by remote sensing to locate geophysical anomalies that could indicate such buried features as pits, postholes, ditches—and even graves. This work was carried out by archaeologist Clay Swindell with our fluxgate magnetometer and by physicist Malcolm LeCompte with ground-penetrating radar (GPR) equipment from Elizabeth City State University's Remote Sensing Laboratory. Both surveys took place in June 2013, and in August 2013, the GPR study was repeated on a smaller area with greater focus.

The one-meter-interval (3.3 feet) ground-penetrating radar survey covered the archaeological site and a broad area to the north in search of features between it and Mettaquem village (fig. 5.5). We located only anomalies attributed to natural cause or modern activities. The half-meter-interval (1.6 feet) GPR, however, more closely examined the core of Site X, an approximately 25-by-40-meter area (62 by 131 feet), and that GPR survey was duplicated by magnetometer. Clay Swindell reported that the magnetometer located several very strong anomalies, suggesting metal concentrations, but also fainter northwest-southeast linear features, interpreted as ditches. Although some magnetic anomalies represented discernible features, many resulted from the plantation-period ironworking activities (fig. 5.7).

More dramatic were the GPR readings. The programming software yields a series of horizontal projections, at multiple intervals, which, due to variable site conditions, cannot readily be equated to finite depth measurements. We interpreted anomalies at the two most determinative levels, one close to the surface and another at a greater depth; both appear to have structures. The anomaly interpretations can be sorted into types according to dimensions and likely functions: historical field ditches and ironworking activities; a possible rectangular post-built structure and enclosure fences; and circular-shaped Native American dwellings and enclosures (fig. 5.6). As suggestive as these images appear, they were interpretative only; excavation was needed to determine the "ground truth."

By 2013, it was clear that our fieldwork and remote sensing had located no earthwork suggesting an Elizabethan fort in the project area. Nor was there evidence of a substantial colonial settlement as that drawn on the surface of the

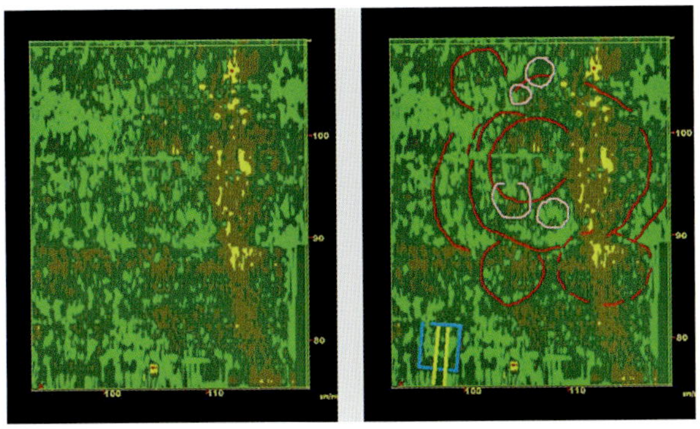

Figure 5.6. *Left:* Mosaic image of GPR anomalies at Site X. Scale in meters. *Right:* Interpretation of anomalies: red, prehistoric enclosure; pink, prehistoric structure; blue, modern structure; yellow, modern fill; brown, geological soil change (*left to right*) and modern farm track (*top to bottom*). Scale in meters. First Colony Foundation.

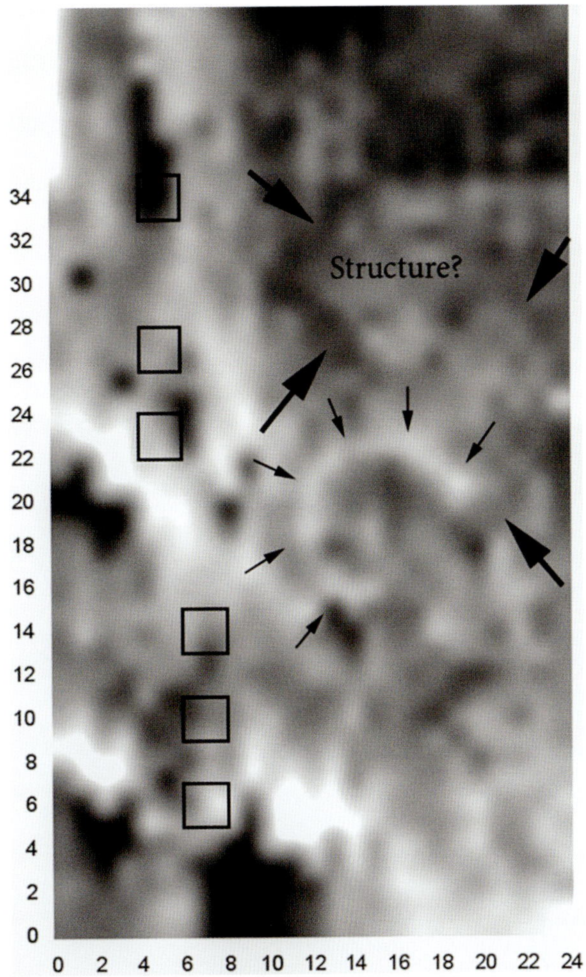

Figure 5.7. Magnetometer survey anomalies. Boxes indicate 2012 FCF text excavation units, and arrows point to possible buried features. Scale in meters. First Colony Foundation.

patch on White's map. But evidence of a protocolonial presence was definitely there, and it may well have occurred in the late sixteenth century.

Yet that was only part of the research success. Before more excavation could reveal details at Salmon Creek, it was already significant to have identified the Native settlement there as the sixteenth-century Mettaquem. The likelihood of an Elizabethan presence at or by that village presented us an opportunity to change the traditional image of Settler versus Indian. Historians suspect that relations between various kinds of colonists and the Native communities and their leaders were much more complicated than those recorded by colonial officials. It was now up to archaeologists to probe one of the most difficult sites to interpret, one where initial contact took place between cultures. And yet the story of Raleigh's colony continued to stir the public's imagination. *National Geographic Magazine* had recently published "One Hundred Greatest Mysteries," listing the Lost Colony among them. Site X and Mettaquem would prove to hold important new clues toward a resolution of that mystery.

Figure 6.1. Image of Bal Gra Plantation along the Albemarle Sound north of Salmon Creek. Google Earth.

chapter six

THE PRIMA FACIE CASE FOR SITE X

Nicholas M. Luccketti

Bold headlines and excited press reports in 2016 told the public about First Colony Foundation's amazing discoveries at Site X—equal to finding the Ark of the Covenant or Jimmy Hoffa's body. But it was only some pieces of broken green and yellow glazed pottery that led First Colony Foundation to conclude that they had evidence of the presence of some of the Lost Colonists.

We do not have a smoking gun—no artifacts undeniably of sixteenth-century European origin. No features from English buildings, no burials. We did not find a fort. Nor did we claim that we had found the site of the main group's relocation or even a large number of colonists. Quite the contrary, we believed that a small number of colonists resided for a few years at Site X—five people and five years perhaps, we can't be sure. And so we had to make the case based on circumstantial evidence. *Prima facie* is defined as an initial examination in which there is sufficient existing evidence to support a case. In common law jurisdictions, *prima facie* denotes evidence that, unless rebutted, would be sufficient to prove a particular proposition or fact. The term is used similarly in academic philosophy.

Site X is located on the north side of Salmon Creek, on a farm known as Bal Gra Plantation. As discussed previously, the site was identified during an archaeological survey in 2007 (fig. 6.1), which was conducted to comply with CAMA regulations (North Carolina's Coastal Area Management Act) for a proposed residential development. A large Native American village site, (31BR189), had been previously discovered on the property. It was known to Raleigh's explorers as Mettaquem (fig. 6.3). In addition, the survey located the site (31BR245) of what is believed to be the home of Thomas Pollock, who came to North Carolina in 1683 and served as its governor from 1712 to 1714 (fig. 6.2).

The survey also found Site 31BR246, which initially was found to contain extensive Native American pottery and some European artifacts. Among the latter was two sherds of English pottery of a type formerly known as Tudor Green but more recently identified as Surrey-Hampshire Border ware—commonly called Border ware (fig. 6.4). The Surrey-Hampshire region has a long history as a pottery manufacturing center, and the ceramics produced there from the mid-sixteenth through late seventeenth centuries are well known to archaeologists and ceramic historians. These kitchen and tablewares are typically glazed green, yellow, or brown. Although Border ware is found on Virginia sites that date predominantly to the period 1607 to 1640, in theory Border ware

Figure 6.2. (*above*) Brick foundation for eighteenth-century Bal Gra dwelling exposed in mechanically cut test trench; inset, detail of west foundation. Courtesy James River Institute for Archaeology.

Figure 6.3. (*opposite, top*) Image locating archaeological sites on Bal Gra Plantation: Mettaquem, Pollock Plantation, and Site X. First Colony Foundation.

Figure 6.4. (*opposite, middle*) Examples of Surrey-Hampshire Border ware and North Devon plain baluster jar excavated at Jamestown. Courtesy Jamestown Rediscovery, Preservation Virginia.

Figure 6.5. (*opposite, bottom*) Image detail showing the topographic location of Site X, Bertie County. First Colony Foundation.

could be present on sites that date to the later seventeenth century. Extensive excavations at the site of Eden House, a North Carolina governor's residence built no earlier than circa 1663 on the west bank of the Chowan River, recovered just four sherds from a single vessel of a late type of Border ware. No other examples of Border ware had been unearthed in North Carolina.

At Site 31BR246, some of the European artifacts found during the survey clearly dated to the second half of the seventeenth century (for example, pieces of wine bottle glass), so we didn't think anything special of it in 2007. It simply suggested that the European–Historic component of the site had something to do either with the presence of Nathaniel Batts (the first permanent English settler in North Carolina) on the south side of Salmon Creek sometime between 1654 and 1657 or with the beginning of the Pollock plantation, serving as a natural landing spot.

Nothing more was thought about Site 31BR246 until three years later when First Colony Foundation asked Brent Lane, then a board member, to see if the British Museum knew of any markings beneath the southern of two patches on John White's map of Virginia, formally entitled *La Virginea Pars*. As Kim Sloan has explained, the experts from the British Museum then examined both patches and reported to us that they had found very little under the southern patch but that there was something under the northern patch that would be of great interest to us.

The discovery of the fort icon in the Salmon Creek area prompted First Colony Foundation to take a second look at the artifacts found at Site 31BR246. Our curator Beverly (Bly) Straube reexamined the artifact collection and found a previously unidentified sherd of a North Devon plain-fabric jar in a tall, baluster shape (fig. 6.4). It was just a little piece, but baluster jars have a very distinctive clay body, and Bly had seen many such sherds during her more than twenty years as the curator for the Jamestown excavations. This was an extremely tantalizing discovery because, like Border ware, North Devon baluster jars are found primarily on early settlement sites in Virginia. Baluster jars were used for storage—in the British Isles sometimes for butter and well known, especially on voyages and at overseas settlements, to have held pickled or salted fish. The jars rarely appear on Virginia sites after the mid-seventeenth century—just when the first Carolina colonists came to the Albemarle Sound.

Given that the Lane colony of 1585 showed strong interest in the Salmon Creek area, the discovery of the fort icon on the *Virginea Pars* map in conjunction with the presence of Border ware and baluster jar sherds at Site 31BR246 led First Colony Foundation to initiate archaeological investigations at what we called Site X, for "X, The Unknown." The location of Site X (fig. 6.5) is near the end of a narrow finger of land bordered by swamps—keeping in mind that today's

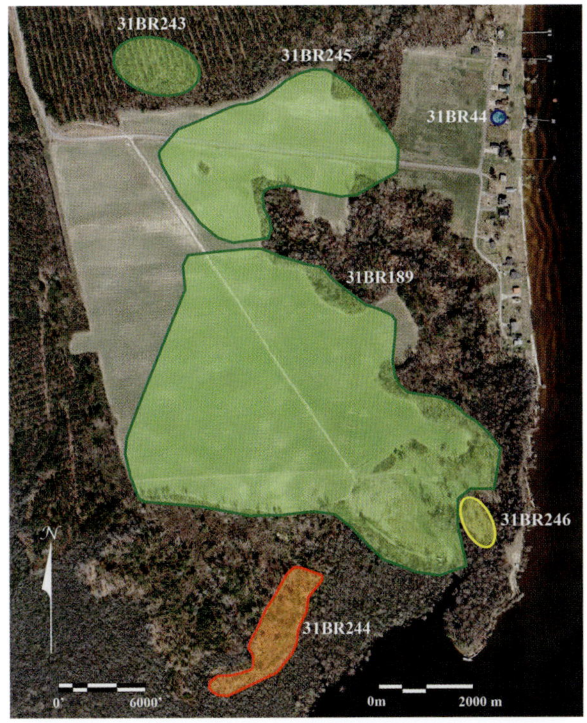

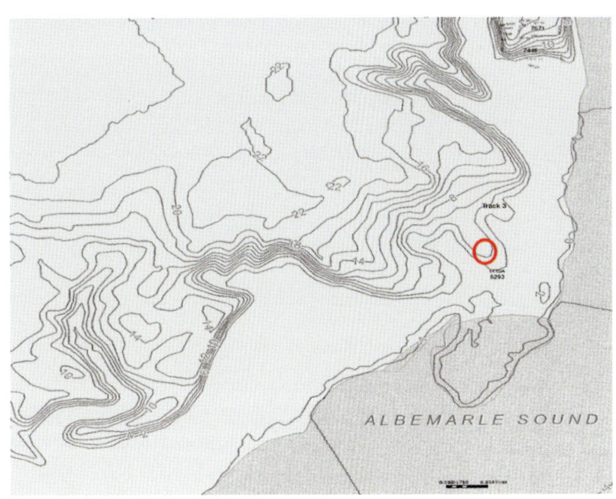

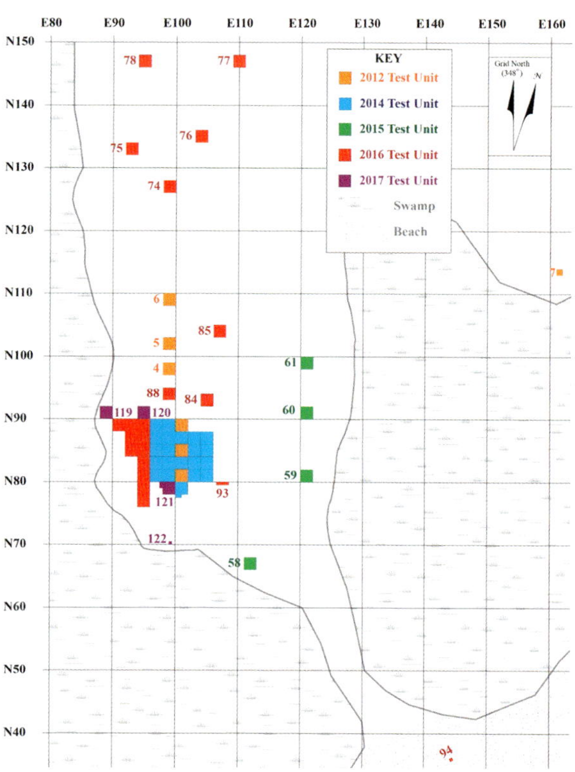

landscape has been much changed by the rise in sea level in the intervening centuries and by soil deposited along the eastern side of the rise.

Excavations began in 2012 (fig. 6.6), resumed in 2014, and continued annually through the summer of 2017—each excavation usually lasting seven to ten days. Fifty-three two-meter (6.6 feet) squares were excavated, totaling 212 square meters, or 2,282 square feet (fig. 6.7).

And what was found? An immense amount of Native American pottery, 600 pounds of it (fig. 6.8)! We also unearthed some historic artifacts dating to the late seventeenth and early eighteenth centuries. But we also recovered more than forty sherds of green and yellow Border ware and eight baluster jar sherds. Together, they represent a minimum of one baluster jar and six or seven Border ware vessels.

It is not only the ceramics at Site X that we think are attributable to a Roanoke colonist but

other artifacts as well, particularly an early style aglet—the metal tip of a lace, for clothing, not shoes (see fig. 9.16). We also found two tenterhooks, L-shaped spikes hammered into posts or trees used to stretch cloth or, quite likely, skins in the New World. In Virginia, they appear only on early settlement sites, where the archaeologist James Deetz suggested that they stretched sailcloth to roof over temporary shelters.

Although we uncovered a host of archaeological features that cut into the subsoil at Site X, all but two of them are Native American pits, and the two historic period features are enigmatic (fig. 6.9). The difficulty is that there is no intact stratigraphy at the site—there are no discrete layers that are exclusively prehistoric or seventeenth century or eighteenth century—all the layers have been homogenized over the years into one layer. So how did we go about making any sense of the findings?

Figure 6.6. (*opposite, top*) Excavation at Site X in 2016. First Colony Foundation.

Figure 6.7. (*opposite, bottom*) Map showing two-meter square excavation units at Site X, 2012–18. First Colony Foundation.

Figure 6.8. (*above*) Sample of Middle and Late Woodland period Native American ceramics from Site X; inset, complete two-inch-diameter "paint pot." First Colony Foundation.

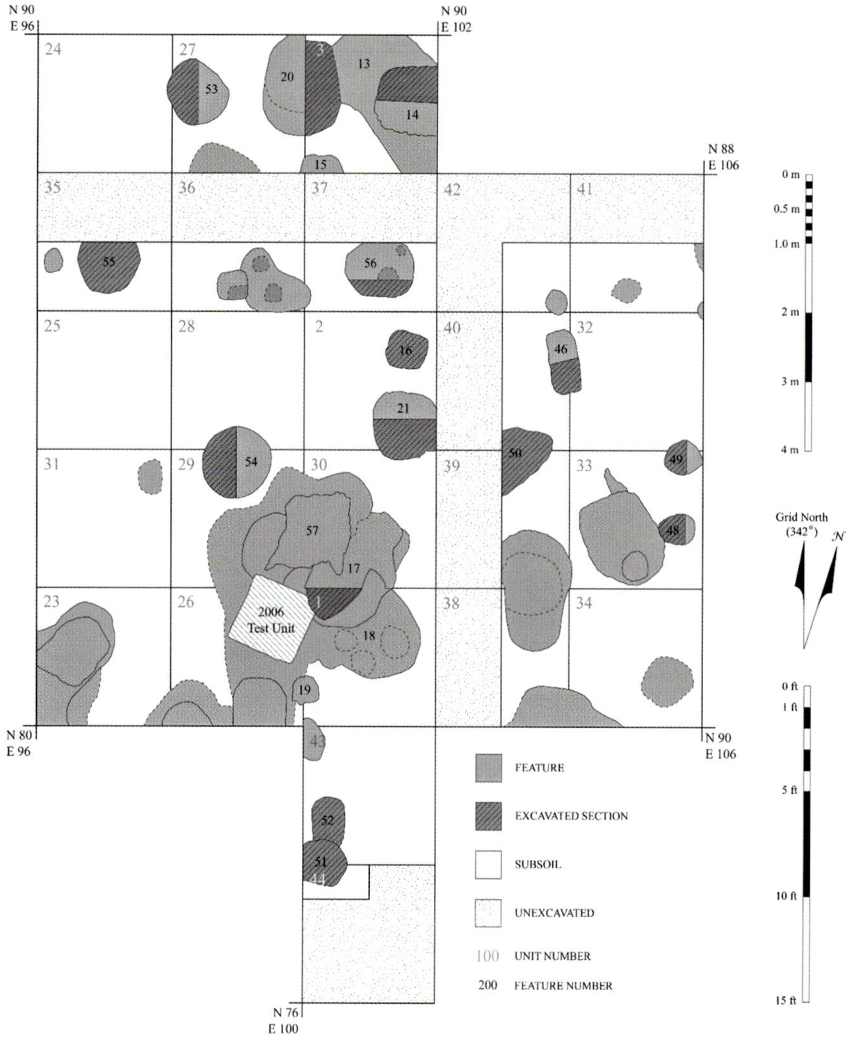

Figure 6.9. Archaeological features at Site X. First Colony Foundation.

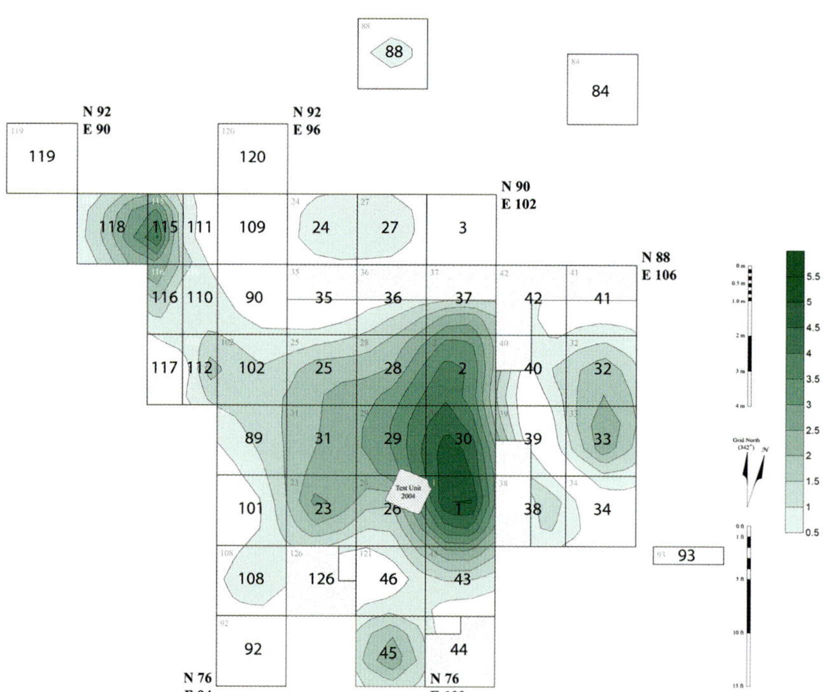

Figure 6.10. Surfer map showing distribution of Surrey-Hampshire Border ware at Site X. First Colony Foundation.

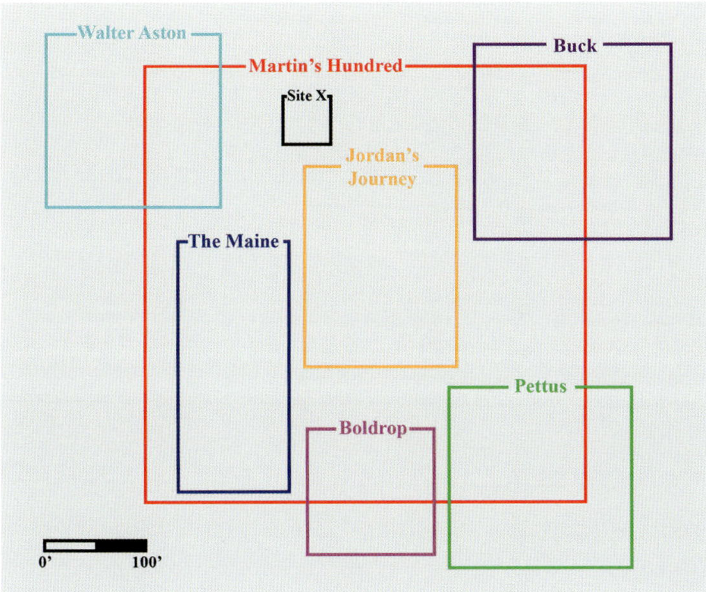

Figure 6.11. Comparison of excavated square footage at Site X to a sample of seventeenth-century Virginia archaeological sites. First Colony Foundation.

We started with a distribution map of the Border ware and baluster jar sherds, which showed distinct clustering in two areas at Site X (fig. 6.10). But although the clustering was suggestive that these sherds were not randomly scattered, it didn't help us determine whether they were associated with sixteenth-century Roanoke colonists or Nathaniel Batts or possibly someone before Batts. What might help, then, would be to compare the findings from Site X with other archaeological sites. The difficulty with that is that there is only one excavated seventeenth-century site in North Carolina, Eden House, established nearby circa 1663. Therefore, to get some idea of the significance of Border ware and baluster jar sherds at Site X, we looked to Virginia, where approximately seventy-eight separate sites predate 1635. Of these, at least fifteen have been excavated, largely during the period 1975 to 2000.

First, let's compare the excavated area of Site X with a sample of the Virginia sites (fig. 6.11). The difference is immediately evident. Site X measures 2,282 square feet, the Virginia sites 10,000–30,000 square feet—four to fourteen times larger! Other data show that Virginia sites containing Border ware not only predate the time of the Batts settlement but rarely occur after 1625–30. First Colony Foundation examined the amount of Border ware at fifteen Virginia sites and the Eden House site. The raw ceramic sherd numbers are a little hard to digest because of the many other types of pottery on these sites, but when you convert them into a histogram, a pattern does appear (fig. 6.12). Most significant are the Eden House numbers, since that site has been used in the past to counter our claims for Border ware. The Eden House site yielded four Border ware sherds representing a single object—a porringer—and they were the later white Border ware, not the yellow and green glazed types common in the Tudor period. We can say that Site X, despite its comparatively small size, has five to ten times as much Border ware as the early Virginia sites, excepting the first years of settlement at Jamestown.

Some may still argue that the Border ware and baluster jar sherds at Site X do not date an Elizabethan presence at Site X but relate to an undocumented conjectural later European presence at Site X in the 1620s and 1630s—and for a sufficiently long time for these colonists to have broken at least seven or eight vessels. We do know that there were several ventures into Carolina country in the first half of the seventeenth

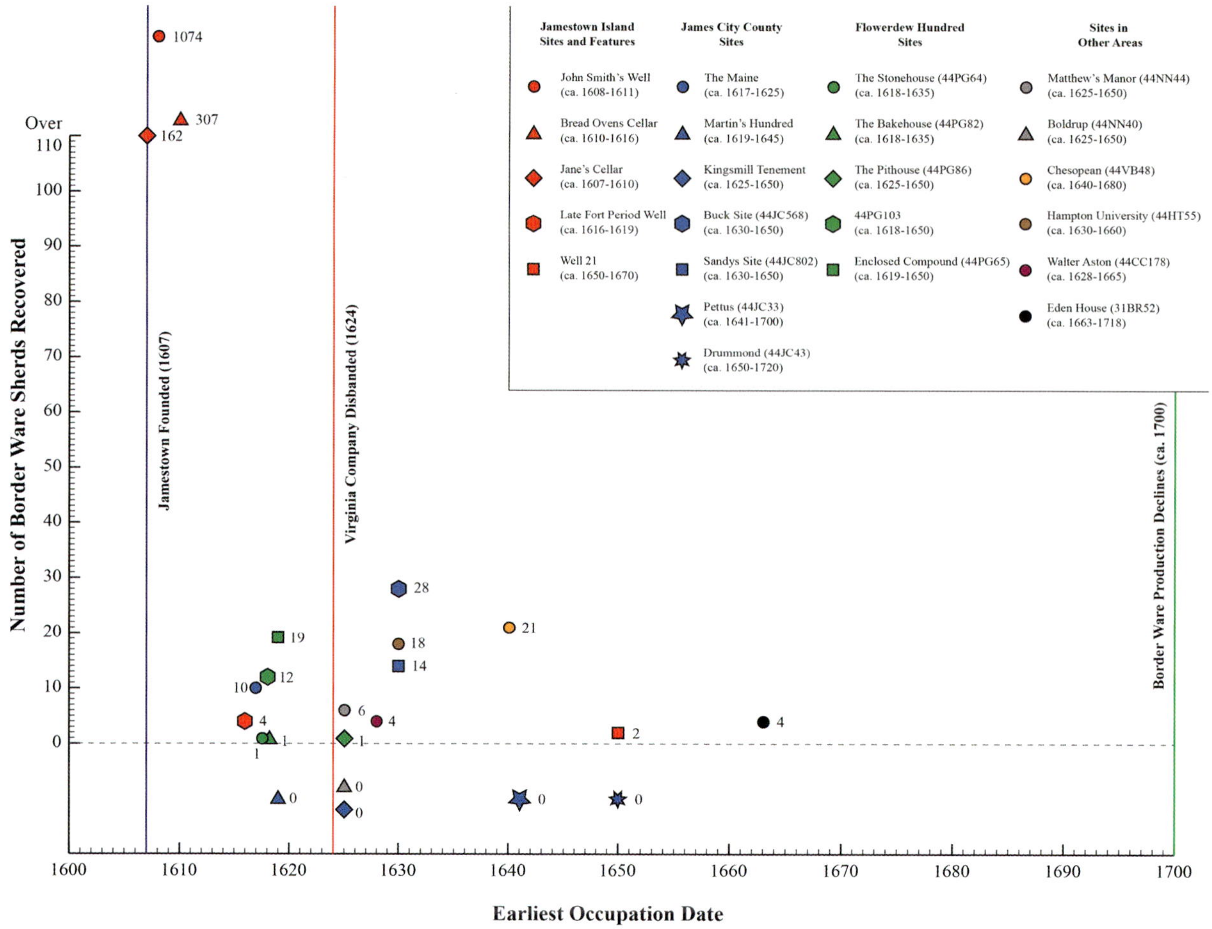

Figure 6.12. Comparison of number of sherds of Surrey-Hampshire Border ware recovered from excavations of seventeenth-century Virginia sites and Eden House in North Carolina. First Colony Foundation.

century, although I find it difficult to believe that any of these brief visits resulted in the artifacts at Site X. The argument that Site X was occupied by someone *before Nathaniel Batts but not Roanoke colonists* fails to consider some basic facts of material evidence found in colonial archaeological sites.

All historical archaeologists can agree that white "ball clay" tobacco pipe stems are ubiquitous at colonial archaeological sites. Such pipes are a long-established principal tool used to date sites. One notable feature of these pipes is that their stem-hole diameter changes through time (fig. 6.13). Tobacco pipes recovered at sites dating to the 1620s and 1630s (see fig. 6.14) invariably have stem-hole diameters of 9/64ths and 8/64ths inches, substantially different from the 5/64ths and 6/64ths inches stem hole diameter pipe stems recovered at Site X. Not only, therefore, is there

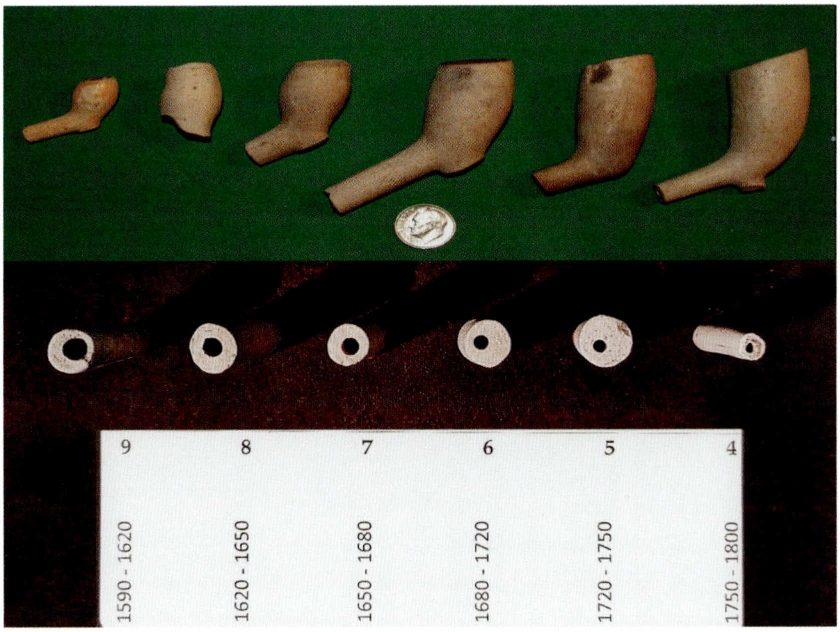

Figure 6.13. Examples of white ball clay tobacco pipes showing evolution of pipe bowls and stem-hole diameters through time—pipe bowls span seventeenth century with ca. 1620 pipe bowl (*left*) and ca. 1700 pipe bowl (*right*). Photo by author.

no evidence of European occupation at Site X dating to the first half of the 1600s, but there is solid evidence to the contrary. Mathematical formulas developed to produce median site dates from pipe stems range from 1705 to 1717 at Site X. Colonial activity there occurred in the early eighteenth century, not before.

Summary

To return to our prima facie case, we can sum it up as:

1. David Beers Quinn documented that the area at the confluence of the Albemarle Sound and Chowan River was of interest to the Roanoke colonists and was explored by the 1585–86 Ralph Lane colony.

2. Evidence of Roanoke colonists' interest in this area is significantly reinforced by the *Virginea Pars* map, which shows a fort icon as the point of interest.

3. The Smith-Zuniga Map, as Jim Horn explains later in this volume, provides evidence that small groups of Roanoke colonists survived in Carolina's western coastal plain.

4. There is no documentary evidence of English residence in this area before Nathaniel Batts circa 1654–57. His house appears on a 1657 map on the south side of Salmon Creek; Site X is on the north side of Salmon Creek.

5. Analysis of fifteen excavated early colonial sites in Virginia shows that the limited presence of Border ware declines precipitously around 1625–30, after which it rarely occurs, and then in minute numbers.

6. The distribution pattern for North Devon baluster jars mirrors the pattern for Border ware described above. No alternative explanation of the presence of Border ware and North Devon baluster jar sherds at Site X has been based on evidence consistent with the findings from archaeological excavations of colonial sites in Virginia and Maryland.

7. If there were an undocumented English residence at Site X in the seventeenth century before the time of Nathaniel Batts, the predominant clay tobacco pipe stem bore-hole diameters should be typical for that period, but data recovered by the excavations of early seventeenth-century Virginia refute

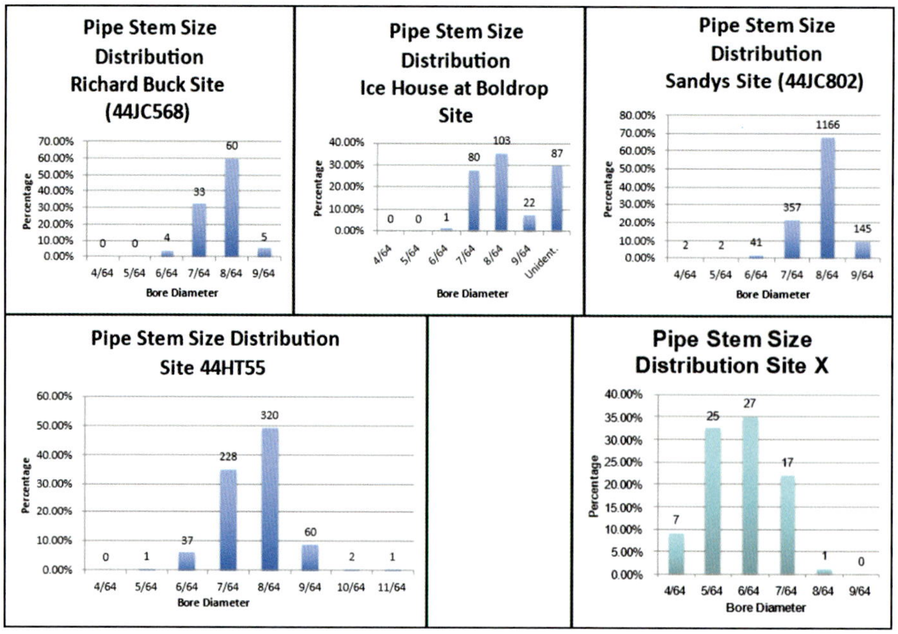

Figure 6.14. Comparison of tobacco pipe stem-hole diameters from Site X to a sample of four excavated seventeenth-century Virginia sites. Graphs by author.

the claim that Site X dates to that period. Rather, pipe-smoking colonists came there only at the start of the eighteenth century.

8. Accordingly, to suggest that the Border ware and North Devon sherds are attributable to Nathaniel Batt's presence or to English occupation of Site X during the period 1620–50 is entirely inconsistent with the evidence.

9. The only known early English activity in the area in question that existed long enough to break at least seven objects is that of the Roanoke colonists.

10. First Colony Foundation suggests that the activity represented at Site X was comparatively short-lived rather than a long-term occupation. Some of us think that it could result from a family unit that chose to live with the Mettaquem villagers. Others suggest that Site X was a sentinel site to provide early warning of the approach of enemies. Or perhaps it served the crew of the colony's pinnace, moored nearby.

11. Whatever its purpose, because Site X is located on the periphery of the village of Mettaquem, it is reasonable to propose that the English there could have used existing Native dwellings rather than construct an English house. It is likely that other Roanoke colonist sites more distant from a Native settlement would have built English houses, using the buildings known to have been dismantled at Lane's "towne" on Roanoke Island.

The simplest and least complicated explanation for the presence of Border ware, a baluster jar, and related early historic period artifacts at Site X is that they are evidence of the presence of Roanoke colonists. Had these artifacts been found on Roanoke Island, there would be no question that Raleigh's colonists had left them.

The Last Word

And so, FCF archaeologists made the prima facie case for Site X. But new evidence to corroborate our case would soon appear. Among the metal objects we had unearthed at Site X in 2017 was a small battered lump of lead. We knew it was the remnant of a bale seal, a utilitarian item commonly used to verify the quality and integrity of cloth shipments in the sixteenth and seventeenth centuries. Stamped with a merchant's mark and a

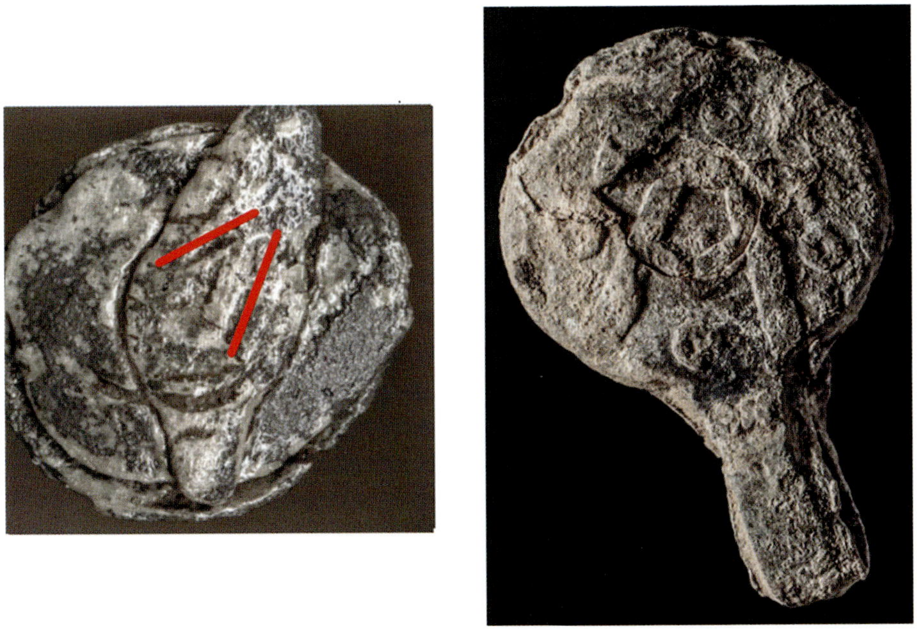

Figure 6.15. *Left:* Lead cloth seal. Red marks indicate angled letter edges. First Colony Foundation. *Right:* Similar seal found in a pre-1610 Jamestown pit, but from a different, decorated stamp and probably later. Courtesy of Historic Jamestowne, Preservation Virginia.

governmental symbol, such seals were generally discarded or melted down after the bales of fabric were opened.

Not until all the artifacts had been cleaned, sorted, and inventoried—a year later—did closer study of the bale seal yield an identification (fig. 6.15, *left*). Though the seal is badly damaged by centuries of plowing and modern heavy machinery, we can see the acute-angle junction of an arm and leg of a Germanic (also called Lombardic) capital "A." This letter form, with T-top, angled crossbar, and splayed terminals, is well known from the monogram on Albrecht Dürer's early sixteenth-century art. The German city of Augsburg was the main exporter of fustian cloth, a linen-cotton weave, and only the "A" of an Augsburg bale seal has these characteristics. With this "rivet" type seal, the conical rivet would capture a corner of the cloth as it passed through the hole in the disk at the other end of the connecting strip; then with hammer and anvil it was flattened by a stamp. The seal found at Site X had been poorly struck, which is why only part of the design appears stamped into the lead matrix. See figure 6.15 (*right*) for a less damaged seal from early Jamestown.

At Martin's Hundred, an early colonial community downstream from Jamestown, Augsburg seals were unearthed at its main settlement, Wolstenholme Towne (1618–22) but not at the later settlements in Martin's Hundred. Some seals were partial strikes, but all had the Germanic "A" with an internal central dot and externally surrounded by small circles. Archaeologist Ivor Noël Hume noted that he had found an Augsburg seal with the Germanic "A" in the Thames River in London that lacked both decorative elements. Similar examples appear in continental Europe, where such a type is thought to end its production before the end of the sixteenth century. Because it shows no other decoration, the Site X example could well be that type. The seal had certainly crossed the Atlantic long before Virginian traders arrived in the 1650s. And that should "set the seal" on our case for Site X.

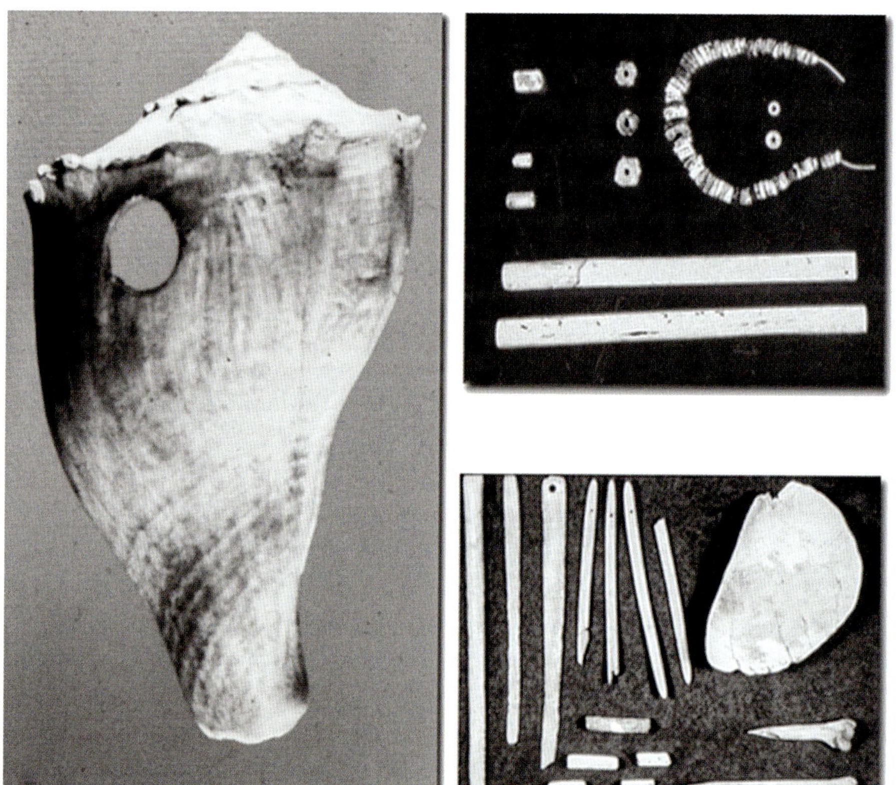

Figure 7.1. Carolina Algonquian artifacts. Phelps Archaeological Laboratory, Dept. of Anthropology, East Carolina University.

chapter seven

THE CAROLINA ALGONQUIANS AND METTAQUEM

Edward Clay Swindell

Most archaeologists believe that the Algonquian speakers of North Carolina were a subgroup of American Indians related to the maritime-adapted coastal Algonquians living along the East Coast from Canada south to North Carolina. Ancestral Carolina Algonquians are thought to have moved into the Tidewater region of the Chesapeake Bay and Carolina sounds circa 600–900 CE and absorbed or displaced the indigenous peoples who previously occupied the coastal zone for hundreds of years. Much like the Iroquoian-speaking Tuscarora tribes to the west, Carolina Algonquians inhabited the Tidewater for nearly a millennium. After European contact in the late 1500s, however, a combination of epidemic diseases, small-scale local conflicts, and regional wars decimated the coastal tribes. As early as the time of the initial English explorations, Thomas Harriot reported heavy losses of life, possibly from measles, in some Algonquian towns. With the coming of permanent European settlements in the 1670s, competition for territory and the rise of the Indian slave trade led to warfare and slave raids, which also took their tolls. By the early eighteenth century, remnant bands were officially restricted to four reservation tracts or had unofficially retreated to marginal environments not taken up by land-hungry English settlers. These fragmented communities languished and eventually disintegrated by 1800.

Archaeology

The field of Algonquian archaeology is based on pottery, tobacco pipes, shell beads, and shell, bone, and stone tools (fig. 7.1). Ceramic smoking pipes, often with incised or "rouletted" motifs, are commonly recovered on late Algonquian sites, as are bone and shell tools, including whelk shell hoes, bone pins, and fishhooks, and an array of beads, ornaments, and pendants made of marine shell or stone, as well as copper. Stone artifacts comprise small triangular projectile points (labeled Small Roanoke), complex worked tools (knives, drills, awls), simple worked tools (scrapers), and polished stone celts (adzes).

Besides these objects, there exists a wide array of perishable materials that survive into the archaeological record only under the best of conditions: household items (wooden spoons and platters, gourd containers, baskets, textiles, and reed mats); personal items (garments, shoes, and pouches made from skins); activity objects (wooden canoes, paddles, weirs, rakes, ropes, and nets); and military-related items (wooden swords, shields, and arrows and armor fabricated

Figure 7.2. Decoration on Algonquian pottery. Photo by author.

from reed). Socioreligious items such as feathers, tobacco, and wooden idols were also perishable.

The most readily datable artifact is the pottery called Colington after the excavation site in northern Dare County where it was first recognized. Based on perceptual differences between Carolina and Virginia Algonquian artifacts, archaeologists locate the Colington Phase (800–1750 CE) of late Carolina Algonquian culture to the Tidewater or estuarine region of North Carolina from the Neuse River northward into Virginia to the southern side of Hampton Roads.

Colington shell-tempered ceramics changed little over time, at least in terms of their vessel forms, which feature pointed-bottom jars and pots and globelike bowls. The pots' exteriors, however, could be plain, fabric impressed, or stamped, and many vessels have added incised or punched decorations. On sites located on the Outer Banks around the time of the Raleigh colonies, undecorated vessels appear, tempered with a fine sand, not shell, and having a burnished surface. Although this well-made pottery was originally considered a trade item from outside the region, recent excavations on Hatteras Island suggest that it represents an internal development, contemporary with late Colington ceramics.

Most notable for the traditional shell-tempered pottery is the unusual array of decorative treatments, primarily in the form of incised and punctuated linear and chevron designs in various combinations, applied to the upper portions of a vessel (fig. 7.2). They are reminiscent of Carolina Algonquian tattoos painted in the sixteenth century by John White and had some as-yet undetermined social meaning (fig. 7.3).

Economy

The Carolina Algonquians were semisedentary fisher-farmers who, by European contact in the 1580s, had developed a complex social structure of chiefdoms. Late Colington Phase site types include capital towns, large villages (nucleated and dispersed), hamlet communities, family farmstead compounds, and seasonal exploitation camps. Homes were typically "longhouses," inhabited by several generations of a family. In the Chowan River basin, archaeologist David Phelps noted that late Algonquian sites are most often encountered on "high sandy loam bluffs along the river and its major tributaries," on land with "larger expanses of arable, well drained soils." Settlement patterns on the Carolina Sounds differed somewhat, with most sites found on well-drained, sandy soils along or near their shores or along the major river estuaries. On the Outer Banks barrier islands, recent survey data suggest that there was seasonal movement between island interiors and their western shores. Similarly, ethnohistoric sources indicate that seasonal movements between mainland settlement areas and barrier islands were not uncommon.

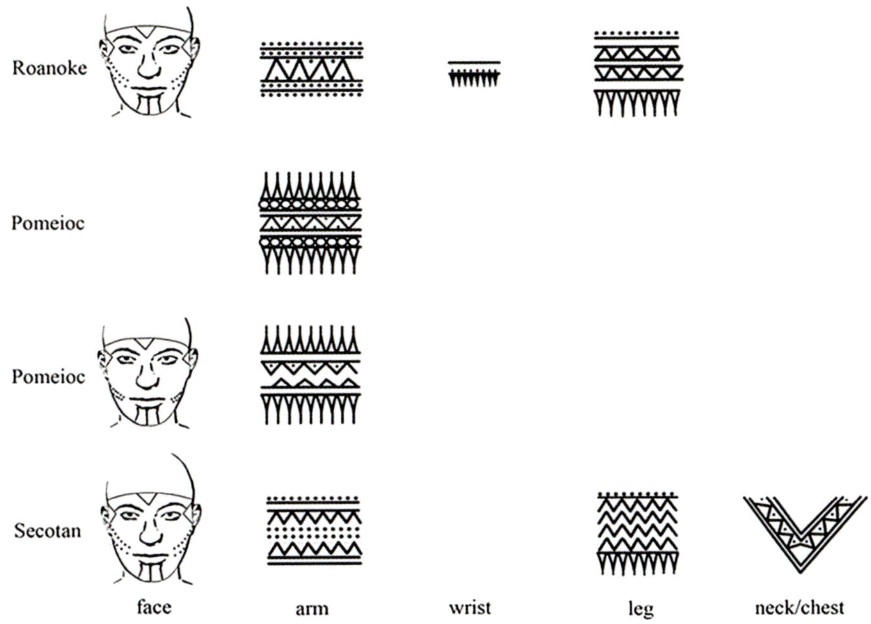

Figure 7.3. Tattoos on John White's Native images. Illustration by author.

As coastal-adapted fisher-farmers, later Algonquian peoples lived near shorelines in settlement clusters that took advantage of diverse marine and estuarine resources while simultaneously occupying agriculturally suitable lands. Like the inland Tuscaroras that the explorer John Lawson described, the Algonquians cultivated maize, beans, squashes, and other cultivars as part of their seasonal subsistence round. Their diet also drew from the exploitation of various flora and fauna. Plant remains recovered from archaeological sites include maize cobs and cupules, acorns, hickory nuts, and squash, grape, goosefoot, and sumpweed seeds. Some studies suggest that maize may have been less significant as a food resource than previously assumed. Algonquians regularly exploited fish, turtles, freshwater mussels, and a wide variety of marine shellfish, including clams, pear conchs, mussels, oysters, scallops, and whelks. Large mammals, such as deer and bear, were probably hunted during the winter months.

Trade

Colington Phase trade occurred most often along the interlinking rivers and sounds. Along these routes would have moved goods, staples, and tribute. From Outer Tidewater localities, goods and staples such as marine shell, beads, and shellfish were exchanged for tubers, deer products, stone, and ceremonial and personal objects of copper. Inner Tidewater localities would have then taken many of these items and traded farther up the rivers for exotic materials like copper.

What data exist on intercultural interaction suggest that some subsistence commodities moved from Outer Tidewater localities inland to localities such as the Chowanoke tribe's capital town (*Choanoac*) on the Chowan River in Hertford County. Excavations there recovered considerable amounts of clam (*Mercenaria*), and minor quantities of bay scallop, oyster, whelk, and periwinkle. Given that these species inhabit near-shore estuarine and marine waters, their presence at a freshwater site such as Chowanoke suggests transport or exchange over considerable distances. Further evidence of such interlocality exchange comes from the Shipyard Landing site in southeast Bertie County, where whelk net weights and tulip shell columella were recovered. Marine shells may have been exchanged by Outer Tidewater localities for Inner Tidewater subsistence commodities of dried or smoked shad and

Figure 7.4. Segment of topographic map showing Salmon Creek area. US Geodetic Survey, 1904.

herring, as well as plants not growing in a marine environment.

There are a few archaeological manifestations of intercultural trade and how this interaction may have transpired. Sea snail (*Marginella*) beads had an important social meaning to the Tuscaroras, whose ossuaries contain thousands of the beads. They would have acquired these objects and others from the coast. After moving into the Inner Coastal Plain by 1200 CE, these Iroquoian speakers produced a distinctive pottery, called Cashie from its type site in Bertie County, most with simple stamped exteriors. Because the Colington Phase type of pottery with simple stamps appeared soon after, it is interpreted as a direct result of cultural interaction. It is not uncommon to recover Colington pottery on some Cashie Phase sites, nor is it uncommon to find Cashie pottery on some Colington Phase sites. This interaction was greatest in those areas where the two populations were closest; in distant locations, there appears to have been no interaction at all.

Politics

The Colington Phase sociopolitical system at the time of contact was described by early English explorers in their own wording as a monarchy ruled by a king. The Algonquian term "werowance" applied to the rulers of each locality who inherited leadership through their status in a matrilineage. Below the royal lineage in this class-stratified society were the nobility, including advisers, priests, and subsidiary town or local leaders likely from related lineages. Commoners supported themselves and supplied corvée (forced) labor for the members of the upper class. A werowance could have multiple wives, likely coming from villages subordinate to him. One polity, Croatoan on Hatteras Island, was possibly ruled or controlled at one time by a queen, suggesting further variability in complexity of the polities inhabiting the range.

Religion

The Colington Phase religious system was formally led by high-placed priests who managed naturalistic beliefs and rituals appropriate to subsistence as well as ancestor worship. Late Algonquian burials include some single primary inhumations, but large ossuaries, containing between thirty and sixty individuals, are most common. The individuals' condition and placement within these dense ossuaries are highly variable. Some have surviving traces of mat wrapping, with occasional red staining. David Phelps interpreted mass interments as the material manifestation of an elite social group, rather than individualized, family-oriented burial rituals. Segregated clusters of remains in large ossuary pits, then, may represent kinship groups included within a single ossuary. Outer Tidewater ossuaries had small, deep circular pits, while Inner Tidewater pits were rectangular or ovoid in form.

Postcontact

Colington Phase local boundaries remain unchanged after contact by the English. Although population decline was likely consistent across all polities, reductions may have had a greater effect on Inner Tidewater landscapes. At these areas, small villages would have struggled most. If Harriot's assessment, in 1588, of death by disease at 25 percent or more in small villages is accurate, then it is likely many of these settlements would have been abandoned or perhaps merged to remain in existence. The number of small farmsteads maintained by extended families would have been drastically reduced, although it is possible that some villagers may have moved out into the countryside. Large open-format villages and capital towns may have retracted toward their political and religious centers as members of the nobility struggled to maintain control. These long-term patterns are conjectural because they place considerable weight on Harriot's statement. Whether populations continued to decline as a result of disease is unknown. Regardless, by the 1670s, those English settlers moving down into the Chowan River basin found large uninhabited tracts of land, and many located their homesteads on "old Indian Fields."

The end of the Colington Phase around 1750 does not mark the end of the Algonquian culture. It simply demarcates an approximate point in time where the loss of core defining attributes of the phase—shell-tempered ceramics, ossuary-style burials, and longhouses—are no longer present. After about 1750, the complicated process of acculturation makes it difficult to differentiate archaeologically the Algonquian cultural pattern from the colonial cultural pattern. Small population numbers are noted for the Chowanoke, Machapunga, and Hatteras Indians after

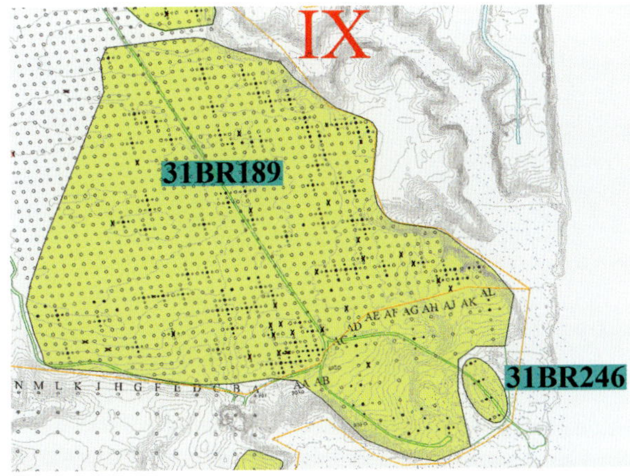

Figure 7.5. Archaeological testing at Site 31BR189. First Colony Foundation.

1750, but it appears that only the more distant Hatteras Indians of Hatteras Island would remain identifiable as Algonquians. They appear to have been practicing primarily their own culture into the late eighteenth century.

Mettaquem

During the late precontact era and at the time of European colonization in the 1670s, the lower Chowan River region was the domain of the Algonquian Chowanoke chiefdom. Sites associated with Chowanoke towns and peripheral farmsteads have been recorded up and down the shores of the Chowan River. Tuscarora sites, identified by their Cashie pottery, have also been encountered, particularly on the west side of the Chowan River. Although such westerly sites likely date to the later seventeenth century, after the Chowanokes were forced eastward across the river onto a reservation, the Chowan River was clearly a fluid boundary between Tuscarora and Algonquian peoples during the Late Woodland period.

The land formation processes differed between inland and coastal sites, yet the resulting environmental and subsistence strategies of the inhabitants were the same. The inland sites were highly productive locations able to support larger populations, and the Chowanokes were thus one

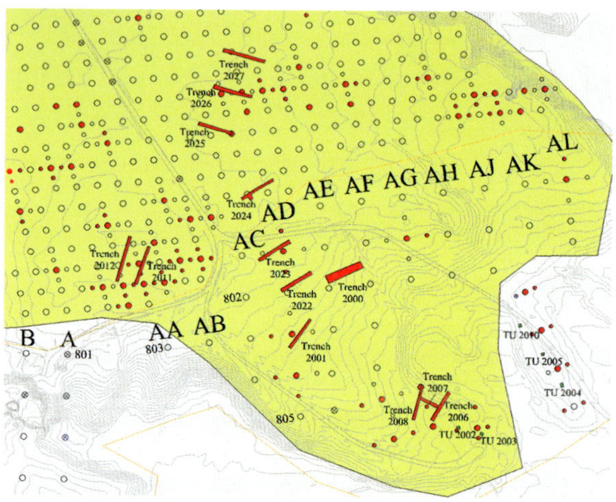

Figure 7.6. (*top*) Mechanical trenching at Mettaquem. First Colony Foundation.

Figure 7.7. (*bottom*) Excavated test units at Mettaquem. First Colony Foundation.

of the largest chiefdoms in terms of population and number of settlements, possibly occupying as many as eighteen towns at the time of sixteenth-century English exploration in the region.

Areas along the Chowan and Roanoke Rivers feature relatively high bank locations with multiple microenvironments. There are excellent arable, sandy loam soils for horticulture and agriculture using the slash-and-burn rotation system; forested oak, hickory, and pine uplands for hunting, collecting nuts, and gathering wood for fires and building materials; and open fields starting second growth and harboring smaller fauna such as rabbits. There are also swamps for items such as turtles for food and cypress for canoes, along with streams and river for fish and shellfish. Easy, protected canoe access in the creeks lead out into the river and sound.

Bal Gra Plantation

In 2007, Nick Luccketti's James River Institute for Archaeology led a study of Bal Gra Plantation, surveying a very large multicomponent prehistoric site, identified as 31BR189 (fig. 7.4). Measuring 2,100 feet north to south by 2,350 feet east to west, the site's general elevation across is twenty-four feet above sea level. Soils there consist of well-drained, loamy sands suitable for cultivation, consistent with other Woodland Period settlement sites. In addition to conducting a controlled surface collection, the archaeological team dug 1,208 shovel test holes, with 231 (18 percent) having cultural material. In all, 905 artifacts were recovered from surface collection and subsurface shovel test holes (fig. 7.5).

I was brought into the project as a consultant for my knowledge of North Carolina prehistory and soon determined that Woodland Period ceramics from all three subperiods, Early, Middle, and Late, were found in the 31BR189 assemblage. Material from the Middle Woodland (200 BCE–800 CE) was most pronounced, accounting for 52 percent of the sherds, with Late Woodland

Colington Phase comprising only 10 percent. The Algonquian practice of shifting settlements within a location over long periods of time may account for this discrepancy. Due to prehistoric trampling, modern plowing fragmentation, and perpetual cycles of surface exposure and reexposure, 26 percent of the recovered sherds were too small or too weathered to make definitive type assessments. Multiple stone tool fragments and lithic debitage (stonework waste) were also recovered from surface and subsurface contexts. The debitage was diverse in terms of geological material and stages of manufacture, indicating a range of stone tool production over a long period of time.

The soil was heavily eroded by decades of plowing, with subsoil generally encountered at six inches to one foot below the present ground surface. Despite this, the intensity of site occupation over the course of the Woodland Period, as reflected in the ceramic diversity, suggested the probability of intact or partially intact occupational features (for example, storage pits, hearths or firepits, and postholes) remaining in the clayey subsoil below the homogenized plow zone.

The team returned later that year for closer archaeological examination by limited excavation (called a Phase II survey). We started with a controlled surface collection of artifacts, plotting the location of each find with GPS. The resulting images of artifact concentrations were produced by a Geographic Information System, which informed us to test locations with the highest archaeological potential. Colington ceramics (800–1750 CE) appeared primarily at the very southern end of the site nearest Salmon Creek.

The team dug seven test trenches in that area of the site, learning that a buried midden (refuse spread) overlay much earlier deposits (fig. 7.6). We also uncovered an eighteen-inch-wide pit that had been quickly filled with refuse, along with another pit that had been left open and slowly filled as sediments washed in after its stored contents were removed (fig. 7.7).

Figure 7.8. (*top*) Ground-penetrating radar at Mettaquem. First Colony Foundation.

Figure 7.9. (*bottom*) Searching for archaeological features at Mettaquem. First Colony Foundation.

Figure 7.10a and 7.10b. (*above*) Two locations of dark soil fill of a curving palisade trench at Mettaquem. First Colony Foundation.

Figure 7.11. (*opposite*) John White, *Pomeiock*, 1585. Watercolor and bodycolor over black lead. British Museum, Dept. of Prints and Drawings, 1906,0509.1.8. © The Trustees of the British Museum.

We concluded that the moderate amount of Colington series ceramics and associated trash midden at the southern end suggests a much more focused or permanent occupation in this location during the Late Woodland Colington Phase. Based on its size and extent, the midden there seems affiliated with a village potentially linked with the Colington material found at four other locations in this part of Bal Gra Plantation. The Colington Phase of the Carolina Algonquian culture included capital towns that had within their territorial control several smaller villages and outlying farmsteads. The total complex here may directly relate to one of these villages situated within the historically described Chowanoke political zone. The Chowanoke king is known to have controlled areas as far south as the Roanoke River, so logically 31BR189 with its larger size may have represented the core settlement of a larger, dispersed settlement. One characteristic typical of town locations during the Colington Phase was their placement along major river shorelines. Though it was not directly located along the shore of the Chowan River, 31BR189 still likely represented a village. Its atypical placement may be owed to the unique sheltered access granted by Salmon Creek to upper elevations where houses and arable fields could be located.

As Nick Luccketti has detailed, First Colony Foundation carried out excavations at Site X from 2012 to 2017, amassing enough evidence to determine the presence of a small group of Elizabethan colonists. But what was their relationship to Mettaquem village, separated from Site X by a shallow little valley or "draw"? Rising waters of the Albemarle Sound and Salmon Creek have made it a seasonal swamp—with snakes—but its western slopes led up to Mettaquem. We had dug test pits in the low land on the west side in 2015, learning to our surprise that the surface was a modern creation, tons of soil brought in to fill what had been a wider basin. So, with a better understanding of the sixteenth-century landscape, we moved uphill in 2017 to where surface finds suggested a focus

of settlement in 31BR189. Using ground-penetrating radar equipment to search for underground features (fig. 7.8) and machinery to cut two long test trenches, we did indeed confirm the location of the Late Woodland Colington Phase settlement (fig. 7.9). But even more importantly, both trenches had intersected a curving linear feature that appeared to our eyes to be a palisade trench (figs.7.10a and 7.10b). If so, Mettaquem would have been a palisaded Algonquian village like Pomeioc, which John White drew in 1585 (fig. 7.11). But further excavation must wait for the future: the property is now secured for the public and protected by the North Carolina Department of Natural and Cultural Resources. Then, careful research planning and secure funding will be needed to reveal Mettaquem village, where we believe Roanoke colonists came ashore and were welcomed.

part four

BEYOND THE TRENCHES

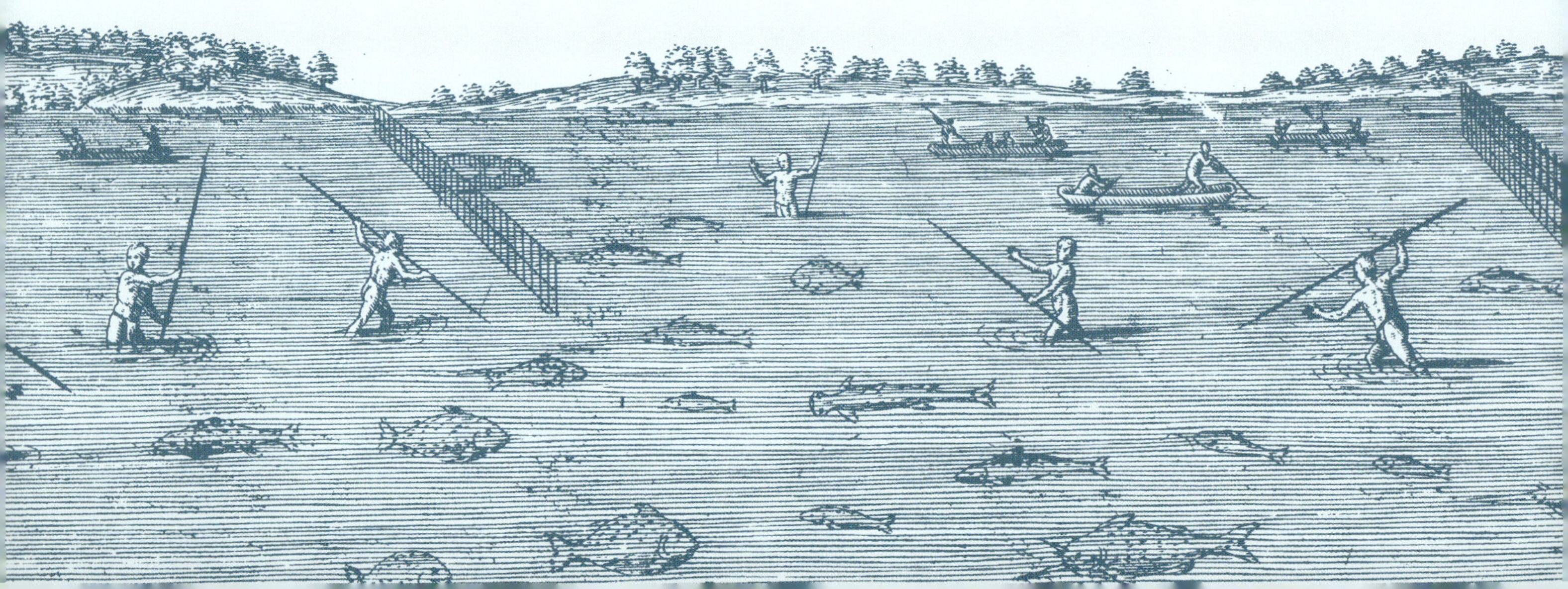

It is time to provide context to the archaeological evidence described thus far. Two nationally recognized experts, one of Anglo-Native relations and the other of early colonial material culture, present their research on the Roanoke colonies. Noted historian Karen Kupperman sheds light on how the relationship between the Native leader Manteo and the Elizabethans provided not just the colonists in 1587 but Europe with unique knowledge of North America and its inhabitants. First Colony Foundation curator Beverly "Bly" Straube offers insight into the world of the Elizabethan settlers by describing the many large and small items that the families would have brought to their new homes in the New World.

Figure 8.1. Title page of Thomas Harriot's *Briefe and true report* with engravings of John White's paintings made in the workshop of Theodor de Bry, Frankfurt, 1590. Library of Congress.

chapter eight

KNOWLEDGE-SEEKING THROUGH COLLABORATION IN ROANOKE

Karen Ordahl Kupperman

When the first party of Englishmen landed at Roanoke in 1584, they were entering an unknown world, but the Algonquian people who met them knew a lot about Europeans and their methods. Giovanni da Verrazzano, sailing for the king of France in search of a sea passage through to Asia, first landed near Cape Fear and eventually moved north along the coast in 1524. His exploration process involved periodically sending a few men or boys ashore to see what they could learn. One of these onshore parties decided to seize a young woman and an eight-year-old boy. The woman screamed so persistently that they gave up on her and "took only the boy."

Sixty years later, Americans along the Outer Banks knew how to deal with smelly newcomers from the sea. The Roanoke reconnoitering expedition of 1584 was greeted by a series of visitations over several days or weeks, and the Native Americans clearly knew what kinds of European goods, especially metal tools, they could get. The official account barely mentions that two of these coastal Carolina Algonquians went to England with the returning ships.

The great question is why Manteo and Wanchese were on those ships. They could have been kidnapped like the boy Verrazzano took. But it seems likely that they may have offered themselves as voluntary knowledge-seekers. Presumably, their own leaders sent them. In England, they could learn about the culture from which the sailors came, comprehending their strengths and weaknesses. And they could shape English perceptions of their homeland and its people. Their venture involved great risks: What if Raleigh's attention was diverted to another project and they never returned? Their search for knowledge and control made that risk worth taking.

Over the winter of 1584–85, Manteo and Wanchese stayed in London in Sir Walter Raleigh's residence, Durham House, on the Strand. London must have been a huge shock for them, so different from the lush environment of Carolina's eastern coast. Over the sixteenth century the city grew from 50,000 to 200,000 people; wood, charcoal, and even mined coal shipped from Newcastle provided heat and cooking fuels, so it was a crowded and dirty place in which to live. Rivers were London's sewers, so the water was undrinkable; people drank beer even for breakfast. During the winter, food was bread, root vegetables, and salted or pickled fish and meat. And, of course, unlike Wanchese and Manteo's people, the English did not bathe.

At Durham House, Manteo and Wanchese collaborated with one of Raleigh's clients, a

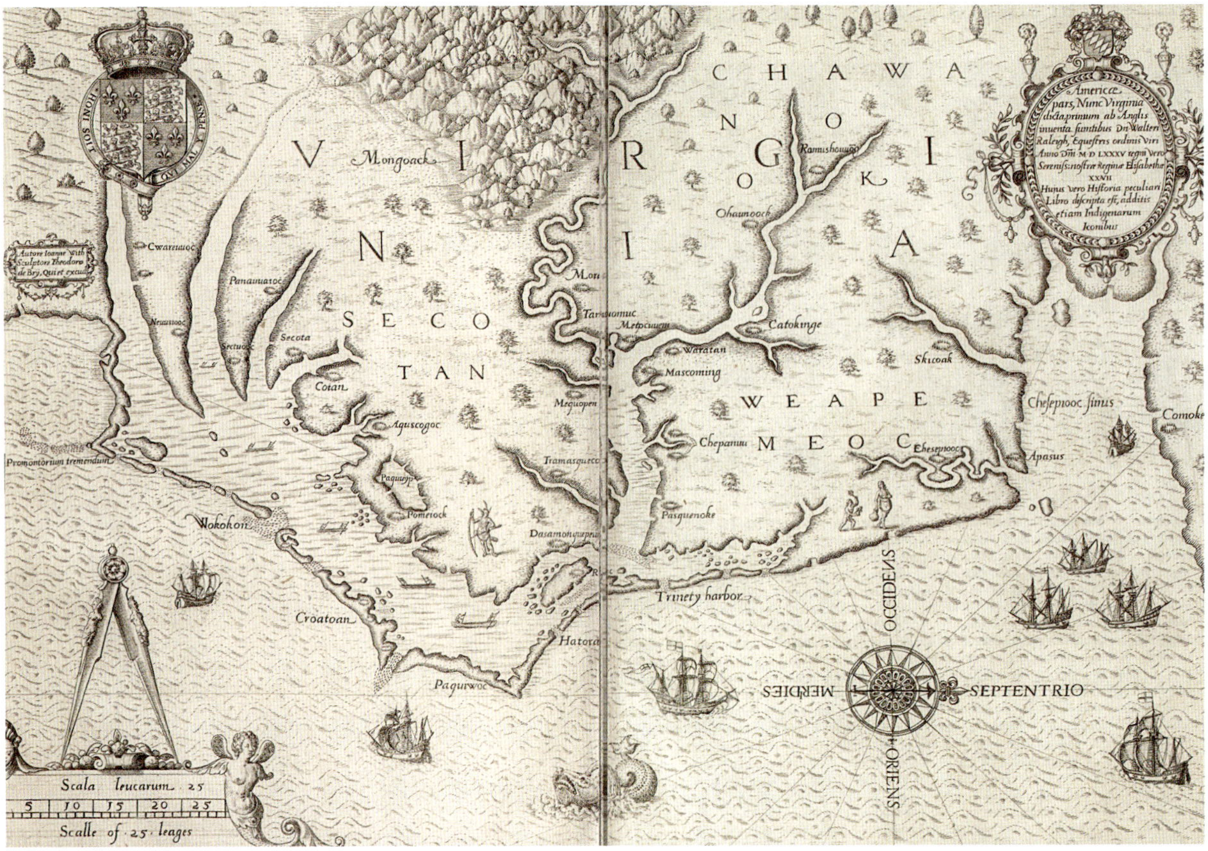

young Oxford graduate named Thomas Harriot. Harriot was twenty-four when he met them; Manteo and Wanchese were young man, so they probably could feel some comradeship. The two men taught Harriot as much of their language as Harriot could absorb in that time, and they learned English. Being able to understand each other—at least a bit—made all the difference for the future.

The 1584 voyage had been a scouting expedition. In 1585, Raleigh sent a group that he hoped would establish a permanent presence on the coast. Sir Walter was interested in the science of the day as well as in empire, so he arranged for a scientific team to accompany the new venture. Manteo and Wanchese's work with Harriot was preparation for that work. The knowledge-seeking team included "gentleman limner" John White, whose job in Roanoke was to create a visual record of the land and people to accompany Harriot's writing. Raleigh recruited Joachim Gans, a member of a distinguished Jewish family of scientists from Prague to supply the metallurgical knowledge England lacked. Modern archaeology has uncovered the laboratory where he worked and discovered traces of the copper from which he tried to extract silver. The team's assignment was to investigate America's resources and produce a full natural history of the land and its people.

Harriot published his *Briefe and true report of the new found land of Virginia* as a pamphlet in 1588. Harriot's text, along with engravings of White's paintings, was published in 1590 by the Frankfurt publisher Theodor de Bry. This book, printed in four languages, brought Roanoke to the European world and became a best-seller across the continent because of the natural history knowledge it contained (fig. 8.1).

Wanchese left the colonizers as soon as the venture arrived on the Carolina coast in 1585, presumably to report to the leaders who had sent him, but Manteo remained with the English. His willingness to stay with the colonists and to help them stemmed from his perception that he could thus act as agent for his own people's interests. Manteo's leadership in producing the team's knowledge was key because he alone could give Harriot and White insider's access to daily life in Roanoke towns and to leading figures in government and religion. His shaping role can be seen both in Harriot's text and in the paintings.

In addition to the *Briefe and true report,* Manteo and Harriot collaborated to produce one of the most remarkable achievements in sixteenth-century science: a new way of recording language by sound rather than by meaning. Harriot called it "An universall Alphabet conteyninge six & thirty letters, whereby may be expressed the lively image of mans voyce in what language soever; first devised upon occasion to seeke for fit letters to expresse the Virginian speche. 1585." Such a system, a syllabary, meant that people could learn to read and speak languages quickly and easily.

The syllabary of 1585 was not taken up by scholars at the time, but we have proof that the idea was sound. Probably the most successful educational experiment in history was Sequoyah's creation of the Cherokee syllabary in the early nineteenth century, which, like Harriot's system, replicated language by sound rather than meaning. A Cherokee speaker can learn to read the syllabary in a few days, and the Cherokee nation achieved virtually 100 percent literacy within a few years of the syllabary's creation.

Recent scholarship has given us a new interpretation of how Manteo's and Harriot's novel system was created. Near the bottom of one page, written in the syllabary's characters, is "MATEOROIDN." Historical linguist Vivian Salmon argued that this referred to Matthew Roydon, a poet and associate of Harriot's in the circle around Raleigh. The new reading of this line is "done [DN] by

Figure 8.2. (*opposite*) De Bry map of *Virginia*. Library of Congress.

Figure 8.3. (*above*) De Bry print of the town of Secotan. Library of Congress.

Manteo the king [ROI]." So, in 1585, Manteo was recognized as the leader in this collaboration.

Another major accomplishment of Manteo's work with Harriot and John White was their map of the Outer Banks, a map so accurate that it compares favorably with modern satellite images of the same area (fig. 8.2). Harriot's mathematical knowledge and White's skill at depicting landscapes accurately were important in making this map, but Manteo's knowledge of the land and water was the crucial element. A few decades later, Captain John Smith produced an impressive map of the Chesapeake Bay and the land surrounding it, and he attributed its accuracy in part to his travels, but the rest was provided by his Native companions.

Harriot and White were deeply interested in daily life among the Roanokes and in their relationship to the environment. Manteo's intervention made it possible for them to understand the coastal Carolina Algonquians as civil people. Civil life was characterized by three organizational principles in European thought: government and law, religion, and settled life showing "care for the morrow." Those who lived a nomadic way of life could not be fully civil. Anyone who saw John White's painting of the town of Secoton or the engraving of it created in the workshop of Theodor de Bry with its neat and abundant agricultural fields, its depiction of the Green Corn ceremony, and its houses organized along a central lane could only draw the conclusion that these people were fully civil (fig. 8.3).

Harriot's text presented an unfamiliar agricultural regime, as he described planting corn in hills with nitrogen-fixing beans around the cornstalks:

> Then their setting or sowing is after this maner. First for their corne, beginning in one corner of the plot, with a pecker they make a hole, wherein they put foure graines with that care they touch not one another, (about an inch asunder) and couer them with the moulde againe: and so through out the whole plot, making such holes and vsing them after such maner: but with this regard that they bee made in rankes, euery ranke differing from other halfe a fadome or a yarde, and the holes also in euery ranke, as much. By this meanes there is a yarde spare ground betwene euery hole: where according to discretion here and there, they set as many Beanes and Peaze: in diuers places also among the seedes of *Macócqwer* [pumpkins], *Melden* and *Planta Solis*.

Using these methods, an English acre yielded "at the least two hundred London bushelles" of corn and legumes, whereas "in England fourtie

bushelles of our wheate yeelded out of such an acre is thought to be much." Harriot was particularly enthusiastic about maize, whose yield he considered miraculous: "a graine of marveillous great increase; of a thousand, fifteene hundred and some two thousand fold."

Recent environmental research has given us a much clearer understanding of those stupendous yields and the Native knowledge that produced them. Carolina Americans girdled trees to kill them and then cut them down, leaving the stumps. The seeds were then planted in holes dug with sticks, thus not disturbing the root systems of the trees and stumps. The pathbreaking research of Suzanne Simard shows the significance of those roots, as she has demonstrated conclusively that trees communicate via fungal networks connecting roots throughout the entire forest. Trees also share nutrients through these networks, so the entire landscape is enriched. Coastal Carolina Algonquians used each plot for just a few years, after which it returned to its own life and new plants grew and encouraged the growth of the fungal networks. Thus, the traditional planting methods made stupendous yields possible. Western science is finally catching up to understanding the "wood wide web" as Native communities always did.

But the assumption that European approaches to the landscape were superior died hard. In the engraving of Native agriculture at Secoton

Figure 8.4. (*opposite*) De Bry print of Carolina Natives fashioning a canoe. Library of Congress.

Figure 8.5. (*top*) De Bry print of fishing and the design of weirs. Library of Congress.

Figure 8.6. (*bottom*) De Bry print of a priest. Library of Congress.

published in the *Briefe and true report*, the engravers "fixed" Harriot's and White's depiction to suit European assumptions. Each plant grows alone in its own field, and plots are stripped of any other plants.

Beyond agriculture, the English admired much of American technology. For Harriot, the single most impressive item of Native manufacture was the dugout canoe (fig. 8.4). He included a long description of the men alternately burning and scraping out the inside of a giant tree to make boats capable of carrying twenty men. Harriot began his description: "The manner of making their boats in Virginia is very wonderful." Canoes were much better adapted to the American environment than bulky and cumbersome European boats.

The English men were also amazed at the Roanokes' fishing technology, which involved intricate weirs (fig. 8.5). Harriot said of the weirs, "There was never seen among us so cunning a way to take fish withall." As long as relations remained good between the two groups, the colonists were fine. When relations became strained, their vulnerability was acute. Governor Ralph Lane wrote that in March 1586, the Native people had an unfulfilled plan to withdraw from contact with the English. Had this happened, "there had been no possibility in common reason (but by the immediate hand of God) that we could have been preserved from starving out of hand. For at that time we had no weirs for fish, neither could our men skill of the making of them, neither had we one grain of corn for seed to put into the ground."

Harriot was also keenly interested in American religious life. Because of his friendship with Manteo and because he could speak and understand the language, Harriot wrote that he had had "special familiarity with some of their priests." Harriot wrote in greater detail about Native theology than about any other single subject (fig. 8.6).

He said that the Americans believed there are many gods, collectively called *Mantoac*. One chief God had existed from all eternity; the others were "of different sorts and degrees." When the chief God created the world, he first made the other deities "to be as means and instruments to be used in the creation and government to follow." The sun, moon, and stars were such "petty gods." The principal God first made the water, and the other gods then made all creatures, visible and invisible. A woman was the first human being, and she conceived children by one of the deities. Their gods were all represented in human shape; individually these images were called *Kiwasa*, collectively *Kiwasowak*. They were placed in buildings Harriot referred to as temples, called *machicomuck*. In White's painting of the town of Pomeioc, the temple is a distinctive building at the upper right (fig. 8.7).

In addition to the priest, John White painted a young man with access to the spiritual world, identified as "The flyer" or "The conjuror" (fig. 8.8). The conjurors, or "juglers," were "verye familiar with devils," who enabled them to

Figure 8.7. (*opposite*) De Bry print of the town of Pomeioc. Library of Congress.

Figure 8.8. (*left*) De Bry print of the Flyer, or Conjurer. Library of Congress.

foretell the future and gave them information about the activities of their enemies. Like the cunning man or wise woman found in every village in England, they used charms and prayers to heal and to help their clients. Their followers believed in them because their predictions so often proved true.

White painted the religious ceremony that celebrated the gathering of the green corn (fig. 8.9). Harriot wrote that these ceremonies drew people from neighboring towns. He also wrote that they offered tobacco, *Uppówoc*, to their gods with "strange gestures, uttering therewithal and chattering strange words & noises," and "they thinke their gods are marvelously delighted therwith."

Clearly, anyone reading Harriot's text and seeing the images White painted and the engravings made from them would have had no doubt that the coastal Carolina Algonquians were fully civil people. It was obvious that they lived in settled communities and practiced highly productive agriculture. Religion was at the center of their lives, and they accepted rule by their chiefs. Manteo had done his job well.

When the first colony made its hasty retreat in 1586, Manteo returned to England with them. He and John White came back with the families who formed the final colony in 1587, and White now came as governor. The colonists included White's daughter Eleanor Dare, and her husband, Ananias. Their daughter, Virginia Dare, was born shortly after they arrived. The colony design was improved because Raleigh now insisted on families rather than a company of men alone, and every family was to have land of its own. According to White, the group was supposed to plant their new colony in the Chesapeake, but instead they were left on Roanoke Island. The colonists were concerned about how they would fare, and they persuaded White to go back in the ships that brought them in order to make sure that supplies would soon arrive. That they did not was in part due to the great Spanish Armada of 1588, against which the royal government commandeered all ships and supplies.

Figure 8.9. De Bry print of the Green Corn ceremony. Library of Congress.

When White finally returned in 1590, he found the colony site abandoned, and no European ever saw the colonists again. The Roanoke ventures made an enormous contribution to knowledge through the work of Thomas Harriot and John White, all of which was made possible by Manteo and his interest in making sure an accurate picture of his people and their land was presented to Europeans. We know nothing of Manteo's life after the English colony dispersed; presumably, his unique store of knowledge gave him a special status.

Harriot devoted his life to science. He, along with the other great Elizabethan scientist John Dee, particularly studied light, God's first creation. Harriot worked on how light was refracted through various substances. He built one of the first telescopes and made many important celestial observations, including being the first to document sunspots. One of Dr. Dee's last communications was to Harriot, and it concerned their observations of the great comet of 1607—it would later be named Halley's Comet. Harriot also made major contributions to algebraic theory and mathematical navigation, and he invented the binary numerical code that is the basis for modern computer programming.

After failing in 1590 to find the colonists from 1587, including his daughter and granddaughter, John White settled on Raleigh's estates in Ireland. The last mention of him in the records was in 1591. Joachim Gans, back in England, was accused of heresy for denying the divinity of Christ, although he had lived in England for a long time and had made no secret of his Jewishness. In fact, he had been teaching English gentlemen how to read Hebrew. There is no record of his punishment, so he may have learned to lie low, or perhaps he returned to Prague.

The joint work of the four men lived on in the many reprints of the *Briefe and true report of the new found land of Virginia*. The engravings of White's paintings were taken to represent all of North America and were reproduced in countless books and pamphlets to illustrate accounts of many different regions. Engravings of the Carolina towns of Secoton and Pomeioc even appeared as Apache towns in an eighteenth-century French map.

chapter nine

EVERYTHING BUT THE KITCHEN SINK

Packing for the New World

Beverly A. Straube

What sorts of objects should archaeologists expect to find as evidence of Sir Walter Raleigh's exploratory and colonizing attempts in present-day North Carolina? After all, in traveling to an unexplored land with no established and reliable system of supply, individuals had to pack "everything but the kitchen sink" to ensure they had all they would need to thrive and be productive. Documentary sources provide some information about the material culture, but descriptions are often disappointingly incomplete or even misleading. The richest sources of data to inform our searches for Sir Walter Raleigh's colonies can be found in the archaeological excavations of England's early North American colonial sites. Even though they date from two decades later, the copious finds from archaeological excavations over the past twenty-five years at the ephemeral Fort St. George (1607–8) in Maine and the more successful James Fort (1607–24+) in Virginia must certainly characterize the material culture of other early English settlements.

One of the most important lessons learned from the excavations of James Fort is to be mindful of the power of objects. Objects have social lives and—like people—accumulate biographies as they move through space and time. As individuals make, use, modify, purchase, sell, break, and lose objects, they give them meanings, and in turn the objects themselves can impart meanings to the individuals who own or use them.

For example, the *façon de Venice* serpent stem in figure 9.1 from a circa 1610 context of James Fort is an interesting choice, especially considering the undeveloped frontier environment for which the individual was packing. He was hopeful, it seems, for a regular supply of wine to show off his status in the colonial community. So fragile and unusable when broken, glassware like this is the most sensitive indicator of wealth in its time. It would be like a modern-day person packing their best stemware as part of their limited allotted shipment for a colony on Mars!

The power of artifacts to signal status, still important even in the wilds of Virginia, is also represented by a silver device primarily used for dental and aural hygiene (fig. 9.2). Known as an ear picker, the dolphin-shaped object has a suspension ring for easy display and communicated to all that the wearer was concerned about the scale on his teeth, the dirt under his fingernails, and the wax buildup in his ears. Most surprising for being so out of time and place at James Fort is a Roman oil lamp dating from the first century BCE (fig. 9.3). Known as a *firmelampe* (factory

Figure 9.1. Serpent-shaped stem of Venetian-style drinking glass. Courtesy of Historic Jamestowne, Preservation Virginia.

lamp), it was made in Central Gaul but is a common find in Roman London archaeological contexts. Was this a practical device to illuminate a gentleman's evening hours in a place where candles were not only impractical but in limited supply, or was it a memento of his intellectual life as an antiquary in England? Emotions can be read into things, especially objects that seem to have no immediate benefit to survival in a colonial setting. It is important for us as researchers to understand the various ways that objects hold value for individuals.

A modern-day analogy can be seen with NASA's astronaut program. Even though it cost between $5,000 and $10,000 to launch a pound of material into space on the space shuttle, each astronaut was allowed to stow a five-by-eight-inch bag called a personal preference kit, or PPK, with up to twenty objects of their choosing as long as the overall weight was no more than 1.5 pounds. What were these objects, and why were they selected above others to occupy the limited space allotted to their owners for the dangerous and expensive journey? Inventories reflect a wide range of material culture from family photographs to playing cards. Some of the items indicate economic value—souvenirs that could be distributed as gifts to individuals and groups who would support the space program. Other objects, however, suggest different values, such as the six-iron golf club head that Alan Shepard took aboard Apollo 14 in 1971 or a vial of dirt from the pitcher's mound at Yankee stadium carried by astronaut Garrett Reisman. Wally Schirra took a Florida hunting license, and there have been teddy bears and baby shoes included in the PPKs. For instance, a replica of a bear belonging to a Holocaust survivor was carried to the space station by *Discovery* commander Mark Polansky in recognition of the plight of the world's refugees. A researcher of the future, not knowing the context of the choices, might surmise that this bear represents the presence of children aboard the spacecraft.

These objects fulfill complex human needs beyond basic utility, which may not be understood without knowing the biographies of the owners and the contexts of their use. Whether of sentimental value, symbols of personal faith, talismans for good fortune, useful for passing the hours, or reflecting a perceived status, such objects carry meaning that is not immediately discernible to an observer even when the objects themselves are recognizable.

English colonists traveling across the Atlantic faced similar conditions as today's astronauts. Small, overloaded vessels, carrying livestock and supplies, ferried them to a strange and sometimes hostile environment. The objects they left behind give us an opportunity to access aspects of life that are not recorded in the written record. We just have to be mindful of the stories this material can tell and learn the language they are speaking.

Ceramics

Pottery is rarely mentioned in lists of supplies or in inventories, yet it comprises a necessary part of everyday life. It also consists of a durable substance that never completely disappears even though it may break into many pieces. Pottery therefore is one of the most informative types of artifact for revealing aspects such as status, patterns of trade, and food production and consumption. Ceramics found during previous excavations on Roanoke Island include Anglo-Netherlandish apothecary jars, Martincamp-type flasks, North Devon baluster jars, Spanish olive jars, and German refractory wares. These appear to be the standard ceramic vessel types marking late sixteenth- and early seventeenth-century English colonization.

Some of these wares were found in an area that archaeologist Ivor Noël Hume identified as the workshop on Roanoke Island that scientist Thomas Harriot and metallurgist Joachim Gans used in 1585. Colorful tin-glazed apothecary jars similar to examples found in Jamestown held

Figure 9.2. (*top*) Silver ear pick. Courtesy of Historic Jamestowne, Preservation Virginia.

Figure 9.3. (*bottom*) Roman oil lamp. Courtesy of Historic Jamestowne, Preservation Virginia.

Figure 9.4. (*above*) Anglo-Netherlandish delftware apothecary jars. Courtesy of Historic Jamestowne, Preservation Virginia.

Figure 9.5. (*opposite, top*) Earthenware flask, possibly made in France. Hard-fired ceramic. Courtesy of Historic Jamestowne, Preservation Virginia.

Figure 9.6. (*opposite, bottom*) Illustration of a distilling unit with a flask-shaped receiver.

medicinal substances for the colony's use and could store samples of locally collected botanical specimens (fig. 9.4). Harriot was engaged in acquiring "many sortes of Apothecarie drugs" in the Roanoke area.

Also found in the workshop are globular near-stoneware flasks known as Martincamp-type (fig. 9.5). They have traditionally been thought to be a product of France, but recent excavations have revealed evidence of a kiln site for the ware in Derbyshire, England. Further research is required on this ceramic type to fully understand its provenance(s). Archaeology has shown that these vessels once had protective woven grass coverings that provided them with suspension loops and enabled them to be used as canteens or field flasks. Their association at Roanoke with evidence of metallurgy led Noël Hume to conjecture that they had been used as receivers in distillation. The shape of the flask is consistent with the vessels depicted as being used in this way (fig. 9.6).

Found with the Martincamp-type flasks and apothecary jars were several refractory clay crucibles—vessels used for extremely hot alchemical processes (fig. 9.7). Like scores of crucibles found in James Fort, they were probably produced in Hesse, Germany, an area well known for its high-quality refractory wares. This investment in costly equipment reflects the emphasis placed on the scientific testing of resources in England's early colonies.

Spanish olive jars have been found at Roanoke and at both 1607 English colonies, James Fort and the short-lived Fort St. George in Maine (fig. 9.8). Most commonly used as containers for oil, olives, and wine, these jars were mass-produced as inexpensive and durable containers for shipping commodities to Spain's New World colonies. The Roanoke settlements may have acquired olive jars through trade in the West Indies, where the English are documented as purchasing livestock, foodstuffs, and other commodities en route. The jars also could have been part of the provisioning in Plymouth, England, which had commercial links with Spain and was a port of assembly for Raleigh's ships.

Also provisioned in Plymouth were the tall earthenware baluster jars produced in North Devon (fig. 9.9). They are numerous in James Fort contexts and are the most common ceramic type found at Fort St. George. Although some researchers have defined these as "butter pots," the form has traditionally been called a pilchard (sardine) pot in England's West Country, where they were produced. They are considered to be victualing containers for dried fish, which has a lengthy shelf-life, making this protein-rich food a long-established staple ration for diets at sea. In 1584, Richard Hakluyt listed dried fish, or stock-fish, as part of the "deade victual" to be prepared for the colonists to Roanoke, and it was still listed as a shipboard food for individuals voyaging to Virginia thirty-five years later.

Even though there are no itemized lists of the supplies that were actually loaded aboard the ships bound for Roanoke, the documentary record contains hints suggesting the types of materials that should be found in the settlements. In 1584, Richard Hakluyt prepared a promotional tract for Raleigh's colonies entitled *Discourse*

Figure 9.7. (*top*) Hessian crucible with copper residue. Courtesy of Historic Jamestowne, Preservation Virginia.

Figure 9.8. (*bottom*) Earthenware jar made in Spain for shipping commodities. Courtesy of Jamestown-Yorktown Foundation.

Concerning Western Planting in which he listed "some of the thinges to be prepared for the voyadge." An indication of what was considered important by the organizers and likely to have been included, the list identifies victuals, incidental supplies, and those artisans and other personnel who would be equipped with the tools and accoutrements of their specialties.

Book Furniture

Hakluyt recommended "that the voyadge be furnished with Bibles and with Bookes of service as well as bookes of the discoveries and conquests" of the East and West Indies. Indeed, Thomas Harriot brought his Bible in 1585 and frequently read from it to the Indigenous people he encountered as he explored the "new found land of Virginia." According to Harriot, the Carolina Indians seemed to think that the book was magical, and despite his attempts to convince them that "the booke materially and of itself was not of anie such vertue, they wanted to touch it, to embrace it, to kisse it, to hold it to their brests and heades and stroke over all their bodie with it."

John White is also documented as bringing books in 1587. These were placed with the rest of White's belongings in a trunk buried for safekeeping when his colony chose to abandon Roanoke while he was in England soliciting support. When White finally returned to the site of the colony in 1590, he discovered that Indigenous people had located his "carefully hidden" chests and that his books were "torne from the covers." As Ivor Noël Hume has suggested, the condition of White's books may have resulted from removal of the copper alloy fittings on the book covers that would have been attractive to the Carolina Indians. If so, they were obviously not the same book-venerating individuals that Harriot described earlier!

Books are represented archaeologically by metal (most commonly copper alloy) clasps, corner protectors, and decorative bosses (fig.

9.10). Spanning the leaves of a book and securing it in the closed position, the book clasp developed from the need to keep early medieval vellum manuscripts from warping. Once paper came into widespread use in the sixteenth century and bindings of pasteboard replaced heavy wooden boards, book clasps fell into disuse because it was difficult to secure the clasps tightly to the lightweight bindings. Book clasps continued to be used for decorative effect and appeared most prominently on Bibles and other religious writings.

Books, especially ecclesiastical texts, were considered necessities for the early English colonies. Traveling to Jamestown in 1607, council president Edward Maria Wingfield left his Bible in England, leading fellow colonist to accuse him of being an atheist and therefore unsuited to lead the colony. One Jamestown colonist articulated the importance of books to those in the frontier settlement when he wrote: "I am resolved . . . to have some good book always in store, being in solitude the best and choicest company." Indeed, more than 100 elements of metal book hardware, including clasps, corners and bosses, have been found in the James Fort excavations. Unless, as Noël Hume speculated, the Indigenous people collected all the copper alloy objects after the departure of the English, it would be reasonable to expect to find book hardware at the site of the Roanoke settlement.

Furniture Hardware

White's reference to his chest of personal possessions reflects the most common item of furniture in the early English colonies. While wood rarely survives in archaeological contexts, chests, boxes, and caskets are represented by padlocks, hasps, keyhole escutcheon plates, hinges, and other brass and iron elements (fig. 9.11). Used to transport the colonists' personal possessions across the Atlantic, these containers doubled as tables, chairs, and even sleeping surfaces on

Figure 9.9. (*top*) Baluster-shaped storage jar from North Devon, England. Courtesy of Jamestown-Yorktown Foundation.

Figure 9.10. (*bottom*) Copper alloy book clasps. Courtesy of Historic Jamestowne, Preservation Virginia.

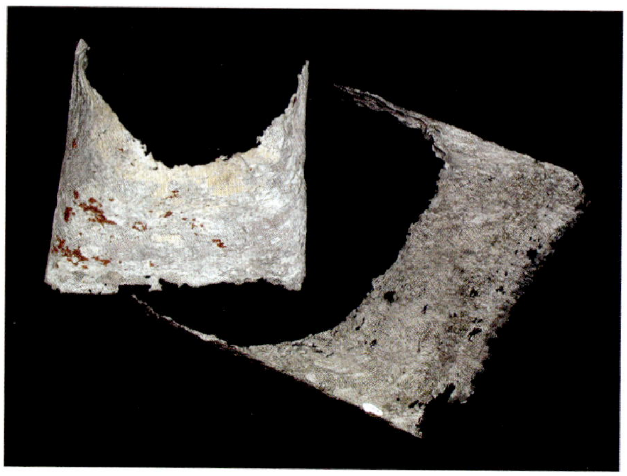

Figure 9.11. (*top*) Chest hasp and escutcheon plate. Courtesy of Historic Jamestowne, Preservation Virginia.

Figure 9.12. (*bottom*) Iron nosings for wooden spades. Courtesy of Historic Jamestowne, Preservation Virginia.

arrival. They also served as the only secure places to keep individual belongings. The absence of stock locks or associated keys for doors in James Fort's earliest contexts reflects the lack of protected private space, which is supported by the architectural and documentary evidence. A similar dearth of architectural hardware would be expected at Roanoke, where the colonists probably lived in shelters resembling the rudimentary cellar-houses, sheds, tents, and communal barrack structures found in James Fort.

Tools

Among other iron artifacts that should be found at Roanoke's English settlements are tools for clearing land, for building shelters and fortifications, and for trade with the Algonquian tribes. A sickle, an auger, and an ax head have been found in the area of the Fort Raleigh earthwork and should relate to the early colonies, although it is difficult to be certain, since the typologies of these tools changed very little through time.

In 1586, Ralph Lane mentioned "mattocks, spades and axes" that he planned to take on an exploratory expedition from Roanoke to the Chesapeake Bay. All these tools are plentiful in the James Fort collection, with the wooden spades represented by the iron nosings with which they were shod (fig. 9.12). The early explorers also knew that it was "needefull to have store of Hatchets to give unto the Indians," who had no metal tools. Made for trade, these tools were probably not of the best quality, as exemplified by the hatchets excavated from James Fort, which were prone to crack at the hammer-welded neck join. Indeed, Jamestown colonist William Strachey admitted that they traded thousands of "poor" iron hatchets to the Virginia Indians.

Armor

Among John White's spoiled goods at Roanoke, he mentioned finding his "armour almost eaten through with rust." Field armor, comprising breastplates, backplates, helmets, gorgets, and tassets, was part of the military equipment supplied to the colonists as protection from hostile Algonquian warriors as well as against possible attacks mounted by the Spanish or French. A planning document for the expedition of 1585 entitled *For Mr Rauleys Viage* states that although the English will be dealing "with naked men," they should have "furnytur to prevent the Invasion of the Spanyardes."

No plate armor has yet been found during the various Roanoke excavations, whereas at least ninety-five elements of armor have been identified in the Fort St. George excavation. Most of these appear to be parts of tassets that hung from the breastplate to protect the thigh. Tassets are also numerous among the James Fort armor finds, indicating that they were probably considered to be too cumbersome during skirmishes with the Native warriors and were among the first elements of plate armor to be discarded by the colonists (fig. 9.13).

A survey of the extensive collection of armor from James Fort revealed many elements that had been discarded, modified, or recycled to suit military tactics in Virginia. Some plate armor appears to have been cut into smaller pieces that could be used to repair the metal-reinforced body protection known as a jack of plate (fig. 9.14). If not properly cared for, armor was vulnerable to rusting and to the deterioration of leather connecting straps, making it unusable. So even if the Roanoke colonists were not adapting their body armor, fragments of it should be found associated with their settlements.

Weaponry

The most common military issue firearm in the late sixteenth century was the matchlock. A firing system of three moving parts, the matchlock was relatively easy to keep in good repair but was reliant on a saltpeter-permeated fuse known

Figure 9.13. (*top*) Iron tassets for thigh protection as shown by the 1607 image of the armored pikeman by Jacob de Gheyn II. Tassets: courtesy of Historic Jamestowne, Preservation Virginia. Pikeman: Dover Pictorial Archive Series, 1999 edition, Dover Publications, New York.

Figure 9.14. (*bottom*) Iron plates that once lined a doublet known as a jack of plate. Image of a sixteenth-century archer wearing a jack of plate.

Figure 9.15. Detail of figure 3.9b, showing harquebusiers at Sir Richard Grenville's camp in Puerto Rico, 1585. © Trustees of The British Museum.

as matchcord for igniting the gunpowder. Also in use at this time was the wheel-lock, a self-igniting firearm that produced a spark from iron pyrites held against a spinning wheel. It had the advantage over the matchlock of being "ready for instant use without the need for live fire," and in contrast to the matchlock, the lock mechanism could be easily mounted on pistols. But the wheel-lock was an expensive firearm that was prone to jamming. By the early 1580s, the cheaper and more reliable flint-ignition system known as the snaphaunce was in widespread use in England.

All three types of firearms have been recovered from James Fort, and all three could have been used at Roanoke. The historical records provide some hints about the types of firearms that should be associated with Raleigh's colonies. In the list of necessities proposed for the expedition of 1585 are 400 soldiers armed with the arquebus, a light firearm used without the chest-high firing rest required by the heavier musket. Arquebuses were indeed supplied for the voyage, as the artist and later colonist John White illustrated some of the soldiers wielding these shoulder-fired arms in Puerto Rico before the expedition arrived in North Carolina (fig. 9.15).

The arquebus could be fitted with a wheel-lock or a matchlock firing mechanism, and the early terminology is inconsistent, with some writers referring to all shoulder-fired guns as arquebuses no matter what the ignition system. From the seventeenth century the term most often referred to the wheel-lock, but some if not all of the earlier Roanoke arquebuses were probably matchlocks based on Ralph Lane's urgent request for a supply of matchcord from Sir Francis Drake when Drake arrived at the struggling colony in 1586.

Documentary evidence also suggests that Raleigh's colonists used handguns. In 1586, commander Ralph Lane described Indian leader Pemisipan as "being shot thorow" by an Englishman wielding a pistol and then later being "shot thwart the buttocks" with a "Petronell." A firearm larger than a pistol but smaller than an arquebus, the petronel was usually a wheel-lock.

But there were also heavy weapons. When he arrived at Roanoke in 1590 to find that his colony had vanished, White recorded coming across "Iron sacker-shottte" left in the palisaded fort, but there was no sign of the "Falkons and small Ordinance which were left with them." A saker was a medium-size cannon, very common

Figure 9.16. *Left*: Copper alloy aglets or lace points. *Right*: Jamestown reenactor Willie Balderson wearing a jerkin with lace-end aglets at waist and sleeves. Courtesy of Historic Jamestowne, Preservation Virginia.

on ships of the period, and a falcon was a lighter piece of artillery. White, however, did see "foure yron fowlers" in the fort. A fowler was a type of breechloading gun primarily used aboard ship. Mounted on the ship's rails to defend the decks against boarding enemies, fowlers were limited to close range. This, plus the fact that the fowler could be easily and quickly reloaded and fired by one or two men who did not have to be trained gunners, made it an effective weapon to defend the English fort from attack.

One of these same fowlers must have been still visible on the site when the ruins of Raleigh's fort were shown to an English explorer in 1701. Along with old English coins and a powder horn, John Lawson mentioned seeing "one small Quarter deck Gun, made of Iron staves, and hoop'd with the same Metal." By the seventeenth century, fowlers were usually cast brass, but two salvaged from the *Mary Rose*, which wrecked in 1545, are similar to the guns Lawson described in that they are "formed of flat iron bars with iron hoops passed over them and shrunk on."

These are just a few of the many kinds of artifacts that typify early English settlements in North America. Not mentioned are the many items brought for trade or the small clothing-related objects such as sword belt buckles and fittings. Or the aglets—the metal fittings over lace ends that enabled easier threading. More than 8,000 aglets have been found in James Fort, where they were used to secure many parts of clothing (fig. 9.16). The hose that men wore, for example, were held up by an average of nine pair of laces, requiring an aglet at each end.

As excavations of James Fort and Fort St. George illustrate, early English settlements leave a footprint of discarded trash. They are characterized by the remnants of objects the colonists used in their daily lives. Archaeologists use such clues to gain a better understanding of the individuals who lived in a particular time and place; in this case, the individuals associated with the exploration and settlement of Sir Walter Raleigh's Roanoke colony in 1585–87. It is objects such as the ones discussed here that have the potential to uncover the presence of the English men, women, and children who vanished from history as the Lost Colony.

part five

FRONTIER AND FUTURE

In this concluding section, two First Colony Foundation experts examine the location of Site X at the west end of the Albemarle Sound as an area of English colonial interest, first by the Elizabethans, and second by the Virginians of Jamestown. Foundation board member and colonial historian Jim Horn explains why the colonists of 1587 left Roanoke Island to settle down on the fertile, friendly shores of the Chowan River, fifty miles to the west. He then ponders what may have happened to them there, proposing that a few colonists lived into the seventeenth century and that their descendants, if any, simply blended into Native communities. Foundation president Phil Evans then provides his second contribution, a history of the seventeenth-century English travels into—and then settlement of—the Chowan River valley. He takes up the story of the efforts to locate Lost Colonists and examines the information those efforts yielded. He then details how that area was permanently settled by the English, with the consequential reduction of Native lands and peoples to the point of extinction. Elizabethan colonists were not the only group to have vanished from the Carolina shores.

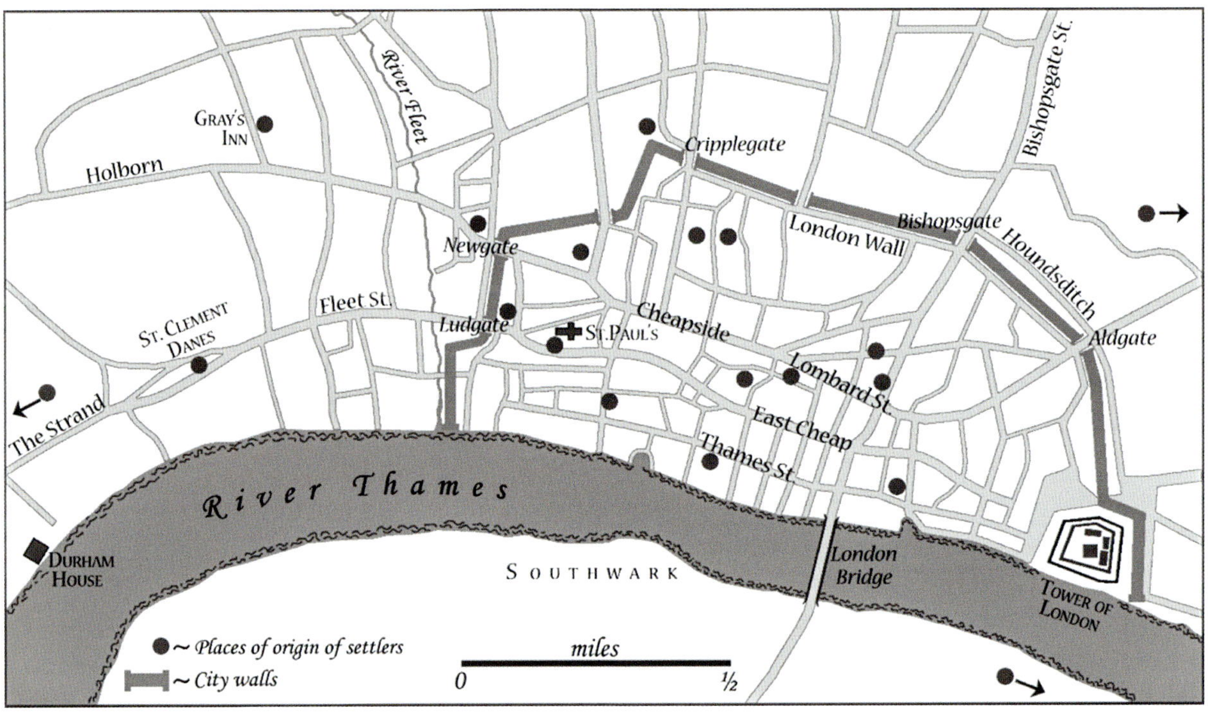

Figure 10.1. London parishes with Roanoke settlers. Map by author.

chapter ten

INTO THE MAINE

Why They Went West

James Horn

There can be few more poignant moments in the history of early English America than the agonizing decision faced by John White on Roanoke Island in late August 1587. One hundred and sixteen men, women, and children led by White had arrived a month earlier. Their final destination seems to have been the Chesapeake Bay, not the Outer Banks, but owing to a disagreement between White and the master pilot responsible for getting them to America, the Azorean Simon Fernandes, they had disembarked at Roanoke. With only a few months of provisions remaining and uncertainty about whether they would be able to obtain sufficient food from local Indian peoples to last them through the winter, the colonists had gathered to persuade White to return to England to obtain supplies and "other necessaries for them."

White adamantly refused, arguing that as the colony's governor his swift return would be viewed as tantamount to abandoning his post. Some "enemies to him," he continued, "would not spare to slander falsely both him, and the action, by saying he went to Virginia, but politikely, and to no other ende, but to leade so many into a Countrey, in which he never meant to stay himselfe, and there to leave them behind him." Undeterred, the settlers continued to press him and furnished him with a written testimonial justifying his departure. One of the most remarkable documents in English colonial history, the settlers addressed themselves to "Her Majesties [Elizabeth I's] Subjects of England" from "wee your friendes and Countrey men, the planters in Virginia," the colonists explained they were "of one minde" in entreating White "to passe into England, for the better and more assured helpe, and setting forward of the foresayd supplies: and knowing assuredly that he both can best, and will labour, and take paines in that behalfe for us all." Deeply troubled, White sailed for England shortly after midnight the following day, unaware that neither he nor any other Englishman would ever see the settlers again.

Sir Walter Raleigh's Men

Little is known of John White's background. He was an educated man, possibly of minor gentry origin, and may have attended one of the universities or Inns of Court in London, but more likely served an apprenticeship during the 1560s with a city master to learn the skill of a limner (miniature painter). Of modest means, he would have earned his living from decorative painting for the rich and fashionable of London as well as occasional work further afield. One of the most fashionable Londoners, and without doubt one of the richest, was Sir Walter Raleigh, at this time in the full throes of his relationship with Queen Elizabeth. Her gifts of lucrative offices, trade monopolies, and other emoluments had made him enormously wealthy, and with his newly acquired riches he had taken on the mantle of England's chief sponsor of American ventures. He knew the queen would forbid him going to America. She would not allow him to be absent from court for long or to put himself in danger at sea, and so White was to be his eyes in the New World. White probably did not accompany Martin Frobisher's expedition to Baffin Island several years earlier, but he did paint—or copied the images of—a Nugumuit Inuit man, called Kalicho, and a woman and child, as well as a bitter encounter with a group of Inuit that occurred at a place the English called "Bloody Point." Raleigh may have seen the watercolors and recruited him on the strength of them. Just as Sir Humphrey Gilbert had arranged for an artist to accompany a proposed voyage to America in 1582 "to drawe to life one of each kinde of thing that is strange to us in England," so White was to paint the landscapes and peoples of the New World, "to describe the shapes of the Inhabitants their apparell, manners of Livinge, and fashions."

Accordingly, White was a member of Sir Richard Grenville's expedition in 1585 that established the first colony on Roanoke Island. Over the course of several months he produced exquisitely detailed watercolors of Indian peoples and their towns, together with the fish and shellfish, turtles, birds, and plants he had seen in the West Indies and Roanoke area. Grenville left the colony in the hands of the experienced soldier Ralph Lane and departed the American coast in his flagship, *Tiger*, at the end of August 1585, intending to plunder Spanish shipping and then return to England. White was likely on board to share the good news with Raleigh of their successful voyage and to show him his paintings, which Raleigh may have wished to use to raise additional funds from mercantile investors in London and Plymouth.

Given what seemed to be the colony's highly promising beginnings, none of the principals involved—Raleigh, Grenville, or White—could have possibly anticipated that Ralph Lane would be forced to abandon Roanoke Island less than a year later. Seeking to justify his actions to Raleigh on his return to London in the summer of 1586, Lane asserted that only the discovery "of a good mine" or a passage to the South Sea could justify the expense of establishing a colony, and he claimed to have heard from Indian peoples that both existed inland. He had been told by Skiko, the son of the chief of the Chowanokes, a powerful people who lived along the Chowan River, that "it was a thing most notorious to all the country" that Indians of the interior called Mangoaks traded to a distant province for a "marveilous and most strange Minerall." The famed province's name was Chaunis Temoatan, more than twenty days from the land of the Mangoaks, and the mineral was called wassador. Skiko described how Indians of "the saide minerall country" panned for wassador in a swift-running river that came down from the mountains nearby, and he reported that the Mangoaks had such large quantities of the precious "metal [that] they beautifie their houses with great plates" of it. Lane learned also from local Indians that the major river of the region, the Roanoke, which "riseth from the bay of Mexico [and] openth out into the South sea," would carry English explorers far into the interior.

The key to Lane's thinking was his conception of a new colony that would connect the Chesapeake Bay to the Roanoke region and beyond. Owing to its shallow waters, Roanoke Island was unsuitable for oceangoing ships, but the good "harborough" discovered there could easily accommodate the volume and size of shipping that Raleigh envisaged. From a deep-water port on the southern shore of the Chesapeake Bay, a series of small earthwork fortifications could be raised to protect an overland and riverine route to the Roanoke River. By settling on the Chesapeake Bay, Lane wrote, "you shall cleare your selfe from all those dangers and broad shallowe sownds [Sounds] . . . and gayne within foure dayes travel into the heart of the mayne 200. myles at the least, and so passe your discoverie into that most notable and to the likeliest partes of the mayne." Settlers would be able to travel along the Roanoke River far inland to the province of Chaunis Temoatan and possibly find a passage to the South Sea "with farre greater felicitie then otherwise can bee performed." The interior, not the coastal area, offered the brightest prospects of spectacular discoveries, and Lane was convinced that by following the major rivers inland he had found the best means of getting there.

The New Colony

By the end of the year, plans for a colony situated on the Chesapeake Bay were well advanced. A major weakness of the first colony stemmed not only from its location but also from the type and caliber of settlers recruited. Lane described the soldiers under his command in 1585–86 as "wylde men . . . whose unrulynes [was] suche as not to gyve leasure to the goovernour." According to the scientist and polymath Thomas Harriot, who was employed by Raleigh to write an account of the Roanoke region, his countrymen were far too quick to turn to violence for relatively trivial reasons. They killed Indians, he wrote, "upon causes that on our part, might easily enough have been borne." Consequently, Raleigh decided that the settlement would be made up of civilians, families as well as single men, committed to the venture. To encourage them to join the enterprise, settlers would be granted 500 acres per individual and families proportionally more, a huge amount of land by contemporary standards.

The colony was organized as a corporation, the *Cittie of Ralegh*, governed by White and twelve assistants as "one Bodye pollitique." The governor and assistants, confirmed in their position by Raleigh and elevated to the rank of gentlemen each with their own coat of arms, would provide the colony's core leadership secure in their authority to undertake the vital tasks of founding the settlement and negotiating with local Indian peoples. They would create the conditions for success and prepare for the arrival of more colonists who would eventually follow when the settlement became profitable.

White shouldered the main responsibility for recruiting settlers. Altogether ninety men, seventeen women, and nine children joined him together with Simon Fernandes, the pilot, and two Indians, Manteo and Towaye, the latter brought to England either by Lane or Grenville. Manteo, who first met the English during the reconnaissance expedition of 1584, visited England the same year. He was well disposed to White's venture, possibly believing that the settlers would benefit his people, the Croatoans. For their part, White and Raleigh believed that Manteo would be vital to the reestablishment of good relations with local Indians and might possibly serve as a representative of the English in the region.

The colonists were a young group. Only White and Fernandes were in their forties; the majority of men were in their twenties and early thirties, and most women were in their late teens and early twenties. All nine children were boys, aged between three and twelve years. Ten couples joined the voyage, four accompanied with (or expecting) a child. Most of the settlers were living in London at the time of their departure (fig. 10.1). Of the sixty-four whose origins can be traced, almost three-quarters were from the capital and about a fifth hailed from Plymouth and Devon. Those from London came from parishes scattered across the city. Thomas Ellis and his son Robert, Joan Peers (Pierce or Pearce), and possibly Charles Flurrie were from St. Clement Danes, just outside Temple Bar, where Ananias and Eleanor Dare lived. Richard Tomkins was married in St. Sepulchre, Holborn, near Smithfield, and James Hynde was from the large parish of St. Giles Cripplegate, just beyond the walls. Within the City, Anthony Cage lived in Friday Street, near the busy market running along East Cheap, and young William Wythers was born in St. Michael, Cornhill, not far from the Stocks, where London's fishmongers and butchers had their stalls. On the eastern side of the City, the parish of St. Dunstan's may have been the home of John Spendlove, while across the Thames in St. Mary Magdalene, Bermondsey, lived Christopher Cooper and Roger Pratt, assistants. Farther downriver in Deptford, Edward and Winifred Powell were married in early 1585.

The particular circumstances that persuaded a seemingly unremarkable group of middling and working-class men and women to leave their homes, friends, and familiar surroundings and set out for an unknown land thousands of miles across the ocean are elusive, but a few clues offer suggestions. Family connections likely played an important part. As governor, John White seized the opportunity to involve his family, who would now have the chance to profit from the New World for themselves. He probably went first to his daughter, Eleanor, and her husband, Ananias, one of the assistants, to discuss the venture. Married three and a half years, the couple already had an infant son and daughter and may have been initially reluctant to take the risk of moving the family but solved the problem by arranging for the children, John and Thomasin (named for Eleanor's mother), to be cared for by relatives. Two other couples, Ambrose and Elizabeth Viccares and Arnold and Joyce Archard, possibly made similar arrangements, but each took a young son with them. After visiting the Dares, White may have traveled across London to see Christopher Cooper, likely a relative of his wife. Cooper had three children under five as well as two teenage sons. His wife, if she was still alive, did not go with him and probably stayed in Bermondsey to look after the family and their business. Similarly, George Howe, gentleman, John Sampson, Thomas Ellis, and Roger Pratt all traveled with young sons but without their wives. They most likely wanted to wait until the colony was up and running before bringing over their families.

At least a third of the settlers were related to another member of the group. Henry and Richard Berrye, John and Brian Willes from Plymouth, Robert and Peter Little, and John and Thomas Chevan of London, were probably brothers. Richard Tomkins, who married Margaret Stevens in 1566, may have been related to the assistant Thomas Stevens. Humphrey Newton was possibly related to Jane Mannering (Mainwaring), and the Tappans to Agnes Wood. Some of the colonists possibly had relatives among men who had been involved in previous voyages or were in Raleigh's service. Alice Chapman could have been the wife of the (Robert?) Chapman left on Roanoke Island with a small holding party by Grenville after Lane's colony had departed. John Gibbes may have been related to two Lane colonists as well as to Lewes Wotton of White's group, and Thomas Hewett was possibly a relative of Jacob Whiddon, one of Raleigh's most experienced mariners. John Wright, James Lasie (Lacey), and Darby Glavin (Glande or Glany, an Irish soldier) were with the 1585 expedition, the only three besides the venture's leaders White, Fernandes, and Captain Edward Stafford.

Other connections are less certain and no more than possibilities. Saint Matthews, Friday Street, where Anthony Cage lived, was the parish of Valentine Beale and John Chandler, both of whom had been with Lane. Anthony was likely related to John Cage who also went with Lane. William Clement and James Hynde, who went with White, may have been trying to put their past behind them after being imprisoned in Colchester Castle, Essex, in 1582 for sheep stealing. Edward Powell was possibly the same man who sailed with Drake's fleet to the West Indies and then to Roanoke Island on board the *Tiger* in the service of Christopher Carleill. He may have been the brother of Captain Anthony Powell, also with Drake, killed in action at the Spanish colony of St. Augustine and described as "an honest wise Gentleman, and a souldier of good experience, and of great courage as anie man might be." A John Sampson, another of the captains in Drake's land forces, had fought alongside Powell.

During Elizabeth's reign, London was epicenter of the English Puritan movement. Puritan preachers established congregations throughout London in the 1560s and 1570s, in St. Martin's in the Fields, Aldgate, Holborn, Smithfield, Cripplegate, Southwark, and St. Clement Danes, where Robert Johnson preached until arrested and thrown into prison in 1574. Eleanor and Ananias had been married in the church, and several other colonists lived in the parish. Religious radicals were coming to realize that there would be no thorough reformation of the Anglican Church, London would not be a new Geneva, and efforts to purge the church of popish practices had largely failed. Possibly the opportunity to worship according to their beliefs was an additional incentive to go with John White to the New World rather than conform to the Anglican orthodoxy being actively enforced by the Archbishop of Canterbury, John Whitgift, who was no friend to Puritans.

John White's Voyages

Three ships—the *Lion* of 120 tons, an unnamed flyboat captained by Edward Spicer, and a pinnace under the command of Captain Stafford—transported the settlers to America. Raleigh's instructions have not survived, but the original plan was for White to go first to Roanoke Island, where he would make contact with the small garrison of fifteen to eighteen men left by Grenville the previous year. He was likely ordered to reinforce the garrison so that Raleigh could subsequently expand trading with the Indians there. Then, White and the remainder of the colonists were to move on to the Chesapeake Bay, find a suitable site for the colony, and establish the City of Raleigh. At that point, Fernandes and Spicer would return to England to inform Raleigh of the colony's safe arrival, leaving the pinnace behind for the settlers.

Departing from Plymouth in early May, White's small fleet arrived off the Outer Banks in mid-July 1587, where the plan appears to have gone badly wrong. Simon Fernandes refused to take the colonists any farther than Roanoke Island, complaining that it was already late in the season for privateering and his men were anxious to get back to the West Indies as soon as possible. According to his own account, White vigorously protested that his instructions were "to make our seate and forte in the Baye of the Chesepiok," and yet he may have seen several advantages in reestablishing at least a temporary settlement on the island following their voyage across the ocean. The palisades of Lane's fort of 1585 had fallen or been torn down, but the houses within and around were still standing and might be repaired for use by the colonists. If, as White hoped, good relations with the Indian peoples of the region could be restored, then he could turn to moving the majority of the colonists to the Chesapeake Bay within a few months.

Much depended on the attitude of the neighboring Indians, and initial signs were not promising. Of the men left by Grenville, only the bleached bones of one were found along the shore. Shortly after the colonists' arrival, one of the settlers was slain in a gruesome manner, confirmation of a continuing hostility and serious risk posed to the settlement from local peoples who had not forgotten the outrages perpetrated by Ralph Lane's soldiers. Without help from the Indians, the colonists' situation was dire: they would soon run out of supplies and be unable to complete the next stage of the voyage to the Chesapeake. Consequently, toward the end of August they made the decision to leave Roanoke Island and move inland, where they might have better prospects, agreeing among themselves also to request White to return to England to inform Raleigh and muster support.

Arriving in England in early November, White reported the condition of the colony to Raleigh. On the one hand, the settlers had arrived safely, albeit on Roanoke Island rather than somewhere along the Chesapeake Bay, but on the other, they urgently needed to be resupplied. Preparations were begun immediately, but by the time a relief expedition was ready to put to sea in the spring of 1588, the threat of an imminent Spanish invasion of England led to a general stay of shipping from English ports. Unable to reach America the following year, it was not until March 1590 that White managed to secure passage for himself aboard the *Hopewell*, bound for the West Indies in a small squadron of privateers, and not until mid-August that he finally landed on Roanoke Island, three years after he had left.

The fort was deserted, houses were dismantled, and the settlers were gone, but carved on a tree near the fort were the letters CRO and, a short distance away, on "one of the chiefe trees or postes" at the entrance to a stockade that had enclosed the settlers' houses, the word "CROATOAN," "in fayre Capitall letters." He could take comfort also from the absence of any sign of a struggle or indication that the colonists had left in a hurry. In case of attack, he had arranged for the settlers to carve a Maltese cross as a distress signal should they be forced to leave, but none was found. The removal of the houses and small cannon, and the burial of chests containing some of the settlers' possessions (several of which belonged to White), which they evidently could not take with them, suggested a planned and orderly move. Above all, the message "Croatoan" gave him good reason to believe the settlers were alive and safe at "the place where Manteo was borne, and the Savages of the Iland our friends." But by another terrible stroke of misfortune, White would not get the chance find the settlers at Croatoan. As the *Hopewell* prepared to sail the following morning, an anchor cable broke and the ship was nearly driven ashore. The loss of the anchor, worsening weather, and low provisions forced the master, Abraham Cocke, to abandon the search for the time being and set a course for the Caribbean, where he intended to winter, returning to Croatoan in the spring. Continuing bad weather and strong winds, however, drove the ship far out to sea and finally persuaded Cocke to head for the Azores and from there to England, thereby ending attempts to reach the settlers in the foreseeable future.

Explanations

What, then, happened to the settlers? White believed that they went to the island of Croatoan to live with Manteo's people. But it is unlikely that the Croatoans could have supported the entire colony for very long on their small, narrow island, which in fact was little more than an elongated sandspit. The leading modern authority, David Beers Quinn, proposed a more nuanced idea. Much scholarly attention has centered on the colonists' words, recorded by White before he left the island in August 1587, to "remove 50. miles further up into the maine," which might imply either west up the Albemarle Sound to the confluence of the Roanoke and Chowan Rivers or alternatively north along Currituck Sound on the first leg of a journey to the Chesapeake. If a small holding party remained on Roanoke Island to wait for White and the expected supply ships, then it was they who left the messages carved on a tree and post before moving to Croatoan sometime before summer 1588. Meanwhile, according to Quinn, the majority of colonists continued their journey northward and eventually settled with the Chesapeakes either at Chesepioc or the principal town of Skicoak.

Reduced to its essentials, Quinn's theory, amplified by Karen Ordahl Kupperman and other historians, rests on the supposition that the colonists would have favored moving north so as to reach their planned destination on the Chesapeake Bay where White on his return would eventually find them. Seemingly adding support to Quinn's argument was another vital clue, drawn not from the Roanoke period but from the Jamestown colony two decades later. According to William Strachey, one of the early colonists and author of a firsthand account written about 1612, "the men women, and Children of the first plantation at Roanoak, (who 20. and od yeeres had peacably lyved and intermixed with those Savadges . . .), were by practize and Commaundement of Powhatan [Wahunsonacock] . . . miserably slaughtered without any offence given him." Wahunsonacock, *mamanatowick*, paramount chief of the Powhatans, the most powerful Indian chiefdom on the mid-Atlantic seaboard, had been warned by his "priests" of a nation that would arise from the Chesapeake Bay and destroy his empire. Strachey wrote that owing to "this divelish Oracle," the chief ordered the killing of the Chesapeake Indians who lived on the south side of the James River near the entrance of the Chesapeake Bay. Shortly before or soon after the first Jamestown expedition entered the bay in late April 1607, the Chesapeake Indians, along with survivors of White's colony, were ruthlessly slaughtered by Wahunsonacock's warriors. Based on Quinn's unsurpassed mastery of the sources, his argument quickly gained general acceptance and in time became the standard interpretation.

Despite the primacy of Quinn's hypothesis, however, a significant quantity of evidence remained that pointed to a quite different conclusion. Strachey, for example, was explicit that the colonists were killed beyond Wahunsonacock's dominions. The Powhatan chief, he writes, had ordered the slaughter "of so many of our Nation without offence given, and such as were seated far from him, and in the Territory of those Weroances which did in no sort depend on him, or acknowledge him," which rules out the Chesapeakes. Other evidence also argues strongly against Quinn's supposition. The first is the meaning of the phrase "50. miles further up into the maine." While Quinn cautions against reading too much into "50. miles" because the colonists were notoriously vague about distances, the phrase "further up into the maine" is more certain, indicating an intention to head into the mainland rather than traveling along the coast through Currituck Sound and then overland to the Chesapeake. Richard Hakluyt, a prominent promoter of American ventures in this period, certainly understood the phrase in that way when he added a marginal comment in the published version of White's account in 1600, stating, "Their meaning to remove 50 miles into the countrey."

The argument advanced here is that the great majority of the settlers moved west. White noted in his account that the majority intended to move fifty miles "further up into the maine *presently*" (my emphasis), which suggests that they anticipated going within a few months and certainly no later than by the end of the year. Several factors may have influenced their thinking. One critical issue was the status of their food supplies: How long would the provisions brought by them from England last? To a limited extent they could supplement their stocks from foraging in the woods around the fort, but they could expect little help from neighboring peoples. If they were to survive the winter and following planting season, they would have to find help from friendly Indians well beyond the vicinity. They were likely concerned also about the probability of further attacks by the local peoples, of being picked off one by one as they went outside the fort or starved into submission after a siege. Considerations of supplies and security determined that they should leave the island as soon as possible.

Yet if the settlers were preparing to leave the island in the near future, why were they unable to identify a specific location where White would find them on his return, and why only the vague reference to fifty miles into the main? The only logical conclusion is that even though the settlers had no intention of going to the Chesapeake Bay,

Figure 10.2. Theodor de Bry, *Floridae Americae Provinciae*, 1591, based on Jacques le Moyne's mapping of French colonies in Florida and South Carolina. The Colonial Williamsburg Foundation. Museum Purchase.

they were uncertain of their precise destination inland and therefore unable to give White any clear directions as to where he would find them when he returned (fig. 10.2).

A possible, though speculative, sequence of events is therefore as follows. When White and Fernandes departed the island with the *Lion* and flyboat in late August 1587, they left the pinnace and two or more "botes" (longboats) with the settlers. Soon after, several of the settlers' leaders ("Assistants"), together with Manteo, sailed in the pinnace to negotiate with local Indians at *Choanoac*—the capital seat of the Chowanokes some twenty miles upriver from the head of Albemarle Sound—about a suitable location for a temporary English settlement. The Chowanokes had been allies, albeit at times reluctantly, of the English in the summer of 1586, and White's settlers hoped that they would now see advantages in trading with them or perhaps view them as potential allies against hostile Iroquoian peoples pressing from the south and west. Meanwhile, on Roanoke Island, the remainder of the settlers began organizing themselves to move, taking down the main timbers of their houses, carefully packing provisions, tools, weapons, and other necessary goods, and burying John White's and some of their own possessions at the fort to be retrieved later. They also strengthened the palisade in case of an attack while they were making their preparations. About this time, they may have decided that leaving a small group on Roanoke Island to wait for White's return was too risky and opted instead to send them to Croatoan, where they would live with Manteo's people. The assumption was that White would go first to Roanoke Island, find their messages, and then make his way to Croatoan, where he would rejoin them and they would direct him to the new settlement inland.

Next are considerations of transportation. The approximately ninety to a hundred men and women of the main group who went in the fall or early winter to the Chowan River area could not have possibly traveled all at the same time. Given that the pinnace was carrying provisions, dismantled houses, arms, and other equipment for use at the new settlement, it is unlikely that more than twenty-five settlers were able to journey at the same time, and even if we assume that they had a couple of longboats, it is hard to see how more than forty to fifty could have moved per trip. This implies that the settlers moved in at least two groups and more likely three or four;

the first group of twenty-five or thirty (including those who had made the earlier reconnaissance) would have been landed at the new site to begin constructing a settlement, and groups of similar size followed as soon as the boats and pinnace returned to pick them up.

Is such a scenario likely? Would traveling overland have been a viable alternative? The possibility cannot be ruled out but is highly improbable. When White returned to the island in 1590, he looked for the settlers' boats and pinnace, which were gone (he thought to Croatoan). Second, an overland route would have taken the settlers through a difficult terrain of low-lying marshes and swamps and exposed them to attack by hostile peoples. Third, they would have had great difficulty dragging their supplies and bulky equipment across the land to their new destination. The English, like Indian peoples, followed the rivers and waterways by boat as the safest and quickest means of travel. Last, the settlers would have wanted to keep their boats with them to ensure that they could navigate the rivers near their new settlement, explore other areas farther afield, and return to the outer barrier islands if they wished. The pinnace and their boats were their lifeline.

The settlers moved west because it was the most direct and convenient route "into the maine," where they would find "freshe water with great store of fishe," and where they had the best chance of being received by friendly Indians, the Chowanokes. Entering the broad, swift waters of Albemarle Sound, ten miles across at its mouth, they would have encountered few sandbanks or shoals to hinder them. Albemarle Sound gave them plenty of room to navigate their boats, unlike the route north through Currituck Sound, which Ralph Lane described as "very shallow and most dangerous" owing to "flats and shoals" in the lee of the Outer Banks and the narrowness of the channel. With a fair wind and following tide they could have made the journey in less than a dozen hours, plenty of time even well into autumn to complete the journey in daylight. The interior also offered greater security from European rivals. Two of their number, Irishmen Darby Glavin and Dennis Carroll, had deserted the voyage earlier on Puerto Rico. White and the other leaders were well aware that Glavin knew the location of Roanoke Island and would report it to Spanish authorities, who would likely send a ship to find them.

Fifty miles westward from Roanoke Island would have taken the settlers to the Chowan and Roanoke Rivers, which would have been an ideal place for a temporary settlement, sufficiently prominent at the head of Albemarle Sound for White to find them. The precise location could well have been at or near a place later described by leaders of the Virginia Company of London later as *Ohonahorn*, where "the River of Choanocki divideth itself into three braunches and falleth into the Sea of Rawnocke," possibly Salmon Creek near the Chowanoke village of *Metpcuuem* (Mettaquem) detailed on Theodor de Bry's engraving of 1590 (see fig. pt.3.1). The discovery in 2012 of fort symbols on John White's map of 1585–86 showing the Roanoke area under and on top of a patch placed at the head of Albemarle Sound, together with Elizabethan artifacts recently discovered by First Colony Foundation archaeologists near Salmon Creek, appears to confirm the presence of an English settlement at the confluence of the Roanoke and Chowan Rivers.

White's settlers likely remained there for a few years patiently waiting for his return, but as time passed and it became less and less likely that he would come back, they settled down and intermarried with neighboring Indians along the Chowan and Roanoke Rivers. The majority likely lived with the Chowanokes and even with the Tuscaroras, a powerful Iroquoian people who lived inland from the coastal area. By the early seventeenth century, most had spent the greater part of their adult lives with Indian peoples. Then, perhaps about the same time as the first

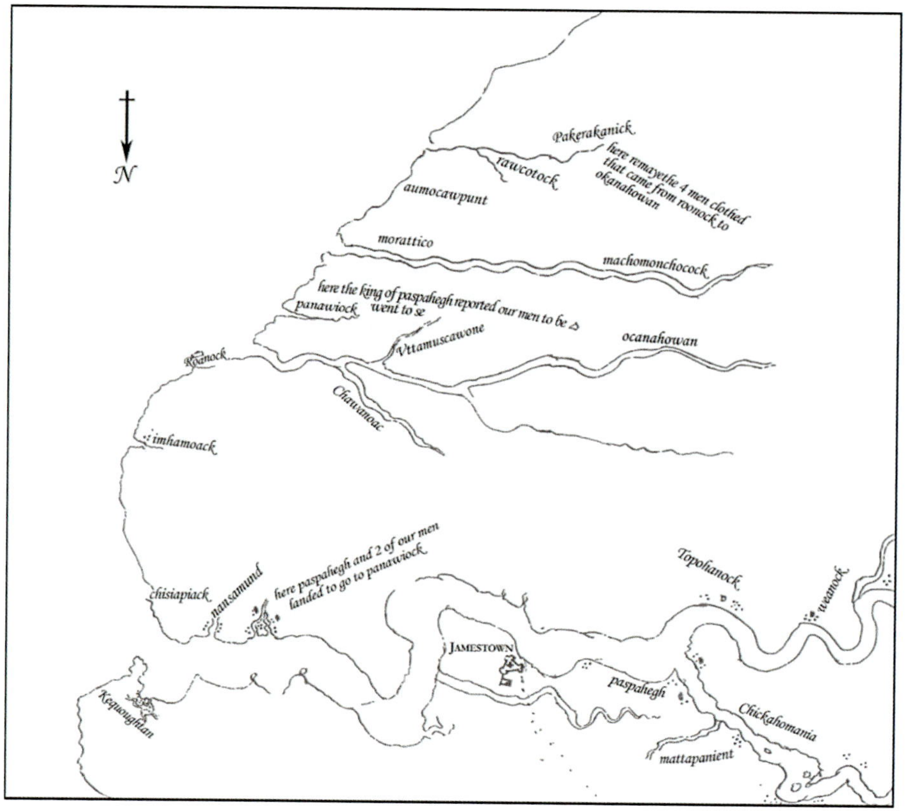

Figure 10.3. Detail from Smith-Zuniga map, drawn by Captain John Smith sometime during spring 1608. North is to the bottom; Jamestown is in the center toward the bottom of the map. His depiction of the region to the south of the James River is vague and likely derived from local Indian peoples. Note that apart from Roanoke Island the entire Outer Banks are missing, as is much of Albemarle Sound. The only contemporary copy of the map exists in the Archives of Simancas, Spain, having been made for Don Pedro de Zuniga, the Spanish ambassador in London. This version was drawn by Rebecca L. Wrenn.

Jamestown expedition arrived in the James River in the spring of 1607, a catastrophe may have overwhelmed them. Jamestown leaders were told that a large Powhatan war party had killed most of the settlers and their Indian kin.

References to the killing of John White's colonists and their children are vague but nevertheless clearly refer to locations in the Roanoke region (fig. 10.3). Detailed instructions given to the acting governor Sir Thomas Gates by the Virginia Company before he departed for Jamestown in 1609 mention a place called *Oconahoen,* described as "a brave and fruiteful" country to the south of Jamestown, which he could make his "principall and cheife seate." Nearby were the rich copper mines of *Ritanoe,* and at *Peccarecamicke* there still lived four "of the Englishe left by Sir Walter Rawely, which escaped from the slaughter of Powhaton of Roanocke, uppon the first arrivall of our Colonie." The information was derived in part from a sketch map sent by Captain John Smith, a prominent early leader at Jamestown, to London a year before Gates sailed. *Peccarecamicke* is clearly the *Pakeranick* of Smith's map, and the place-name *Oconahoen* or *Ocanahonan* had been related to Smith in earlier conversations with Wahunsonacock and his powerful kinsman Opechancanough.

A detailed consideration of the reasons why Wahunsonacock would have ordered the destruction of survivors from White's colony and their Indian allies is unnecessary here. They could have been victims of fighting along an unstable border zone between three major peoples vying for regional dominance—the Powhatans, Tuscaroras, and Chowanokes—that escalated into open conflict with the arrival of the Jamestown colony. Evidence of English survivors living in the North Carolina interior offers a strong argument, however, that the settlers initially moved west from Roanoke Island before moving farther inland.

Survival?

The men and women of London, Plymouth, and other parts of southern England recruited by John White to establish a colony in Virginia never reached the Chesapeake Bay; they never established a great city in Raleigh's name or discovered gold mines in the distant province of Chaunis Temoatan. A North American El Dorado did not lie in the mountains, and there was no convenient water passage that would take the English through the landmass to the South Sea and Cathay. The settlers could not have possibly anticipated the adversities faced by John White after he left for England in 1587 that prevented him from returning to Roanoke Island, but following his failure to come back with supplies and reinforcements, they turned to local peoples for help. How many could have survived the calamity of a war along the Chowan and Roanoke Rivers is uncertain. An Indian named Machumps, one of William Strachey's sources, told him that seven (four Englishmen and three children, most likely Anglo-Indian) were protected by a powerful chief, Eyanoco, an "enemy to Powhaton," and beat his copper at Ritanoe deep in the interior near the mountains. Others also escaped and lived with Tuscarora peoples at Panawicke, Ocanahonan, and Pakerakanick, where they built "walled" houses like those of the English. Roanoke Island was no longer home, but perhaps a dozen still lived on Croatoan Island with Manteo's people, oblivious of what had become of their compatriots inland. Perhaps like their distant friends in the west, those that survived did so by blending into Indian communities, making their homes and raising families with the peoples they found when they were lost to the English.

A Note on Sources

Of 118 colonists, a parish of baptism or marriage was identified for 64, of which 46 were from London and its suburbs. Anyone researching the English backgrounds of the Lost Colonies owes an enormous debt to the pioneering work of William S. Powell and more recently lebame houston and Olivia A. Isil. I am grateful to lebame houston for generously sharing her unpublished work and to Dr. Susan Shames, formerly of the John D. Rockefeller Jr. Library of the Colonial Williamsburg Foundation, for her meticulous research. Names of the colonists were checked against the online International Genealogical Index of the Church of Jesus Christ of Latter-day Saints. They were cross-checked against parish records and printed sources including the *Harleian Society*, vols. 1–81, and Joseph Lemuel Chester, ed., *Allegations for Marriage Licenses Issued by the Bishop of London, 1520 to 1610* (London, 1887). Manuscript parish records were checked at the London Metropolitan Archives, the Guildhall Library, and the City of Westminster Archives in London. At the Outer Banks History Center, Manteo, North Carolina, are several dozen boxes of materials relating to research undertaken in London archives by houston and Isil as well as unpublished materials by Powell.

Figure 11.1. John Smith's depiction of his capture by Natives, from his *General History of Virginia, New England, and the Summer Isles*, 1624. Special Collections, John D. Rockefeller Jr. Library, The Colonial Williamsburg Foundation.

chapter eleven

THE ENGLISH ON THE CHOWAN

Phillip W. Evans

The Chowan River basin first appears in the historical record of English exploration and colonization of America in 1584 with the report of Arthur Barlowe on the first of the voyages made under a charter Queen Elizabeth I granted to Walter Raleigh that same year (see fig. 1.1). Between the time of that reference and the documented, permanent English settlement of the Chowan River basin in the third quarter of the seventeenth century, there are several instances where reports of English interest and presence in the region are still extant. What we know from the written record may need to be augmented by the archaeological record.

Early Contact, 1584–86

In 1584, Barlowe wrote that the English were informed that a "great Towne, called Chowanoake," stood beside a river called Nomopana. It is not clear whether this Nomopana was a name for the Chowan River, a name for the northern shore of what is now Albemarle Sound, or a name for the confluence of the modern Chowan and Roanoke Rivers. Barlowe further reported that "the Lorde of that Towne and Country, is called Pooneno: this Pooneno is not subject to the King of Wingandacoa, but is a free Lorde." Barlowe went on to write that "beyonde this countrey (Chowanoake), is there another King, whome they call Menatoan." Pooneno did not reappear in the accounts of the Roanoke voyages, and it is difficult understand whether he was of the Chowanoke, Weapemeoc, or Moratuc tribe. Menatoan or Menatonan was prominently mentioned in the accounts of the English exploration of the Chowan in 1586. Barlowe tried to make clear that Pooneno and Menatonan were independent allies and not subjects of Wingina, the reported "king" of Wingandacoa. The English believed that Wingandacoa was the name of the region stretching from Roanoke Island southwest to Secotan on or near the modern Pamlico Sound.

Under the continued sponsorship of the newly knighted Sir Walter Raleigh, the English returned to the region in the summer of 1585. They proceeded to establish a colony in the newly named "Virginia," as well as to venture from Roanoke Island up the modern Albemarle Sound. The journal of the H.M.S. *Tiger* records that on August 2, 1585, "The Admirall was sent to Weapemeoke" on the north shore of that waterway. The admiral here was likely not the flagship, the *Tiger*, because that vessel would almost certainly have drawn too much water for entrance into Roanoke Sound for exploration. The term

"Admirall" referred to Philip Amadas, who was listed as the "Admirall of the countrie." Amadas had commanded with Barlowe the voyage the year before. He probably sailed one of the single-masted pinnaces that were part of the small fleet commanded by Sir Richard Grenville, and he is believed to have returned to Roanoke Island before September 8, 1585. How far up the sound Amadas went and what was done there is not recorded. Amadas remained with the Roanoke Island colony under the command of Ralph Lane after Grenville's return to England (see figs. 4.4a and 4.4b). Information on any additional exploration of the Chowan region in the fall and winter of 1585–86 is not extant. In reporting on his adventure up the Roanoke River in spring 1586, Ralph Lane wrote that the *Moratiks* (Moratucs) abandoned their towns even though "they had ever dealt kindly with us," which suggests that some interaction had occurred in the preceding months. Lane attributed the unexpected retreat of the Moratucs and the neighboring Mangoaks to the machinations of Wingina and not to any previous conflicts between the English and the inhabitants of the lands along the Roanoke River.

Lane's voyage of exploration partially up both the Chowan and Roanoke Rivers in 1586 was very eventful and extremely informative for the English. Lane stated that Menatonan, the "King" of the Chowanokes, "gave me more understanding and light of the Country then I had received by all the searches and salvages that before I or any of my companie had had conference with." Lane's complete narrative of the exploration will not be recounted here, but it is important to note that he describes the region in considerable detail ("I have set downe this voyage somewhat particularly") and strongly argues for future exploration for "the discovery of a good mine . . . or a passage to the Southsea, or some way to it." Lane further stated that only discovery of either one of these would make the other potential commodities to be raised or collected really worth the cost of their shipping.

Part of Lane's discourse on his exploration outlines his plan to search out the bay with a good harbor reported to be north of the Chowan. Lane and Menatonan had discussed this in their conferences. Lane thought that "a mayne forte" on this bay could be connected with the upper reaches ("the head of the River") of the Chowan by a series of sconces (small earthwork forts). Each sconce would be topped by a palisade and be sited at a cornfield, which suggests he intended to place them adjacent to small Native towns or hamlets. He also intended to keep boats on the Chowan River so that he could both maintain the connection with Roanoke Island and continue the exploration of the Roanoke (Moratuc) River.

Lane was unable to carry out this plan in the spring and summer of 1586. The failure of Raleigh's supply vessels to arrive as early as they had been promised, conflict in late May and early June with the Roanoke tribe, and the arrival of Sir Francis Drake on a storm-tossed sea all combined to conclude the first English colony, with its planned explorations into the interior, with a somewhat precipitate embarkation for a return voyage to England. Drake's ships (with Lane's colonists) were barely over the eastern horizon when a supply ship from Raleigh arrived. There is no record that its crew ventured into the interior. Shortly after their departure, Sir Richard Grenville arrived. He is reported to have traveled "up into divers places of the Countrie before deciding to land fifteen men with all maner of provision for two yeeres" on Roanoke Island before returning to England.

Into the Maine, 1587 and 1590

When another group of English colonists arrived in Raleigh's Virginia, they included not just men but women and children. They found no survivors from the party of fifteen men left by Grenville. About a month after their arrival in late July 1587, these people became anxious for someone to return to England to oversee their resupply in 1588, and they pressed their governor, John White, to do this. Afterward, he set sail back to England, but no other specific information on the destination was given. When White eventually returned in August 1590, he found the word "CROATOAN" carved at a palisade. Although this did not indicate removal to a site fifty miles into the mainland, White again noted that had been the intent of the colonists in 1587.

Post-Roanoke and Pre-Jamestown Contacts, 1590–1606

No record survives of searches for the colony between 1590 and 1602. In the latter year, Samuel Mace made a voyage for Sir Walter Raleigh, but he did not come into the area of the Chowan or Roanoke Rivers. Mace made another voyage in 1603, but no record survives of what occurred on the voyage or where Mace might have landed. A near contemporaneous voyage by Bartholomew Gilbert does not appear to have come any closer than the mouth of the Chesapeake Bay. Gilbert was reported unable to enter the bay and was later killed somewhere on the Atlantic shore to the north of modern Cape Charles, Virginia.

Throughout the documentation of this early period of exploration and colonization there was a continual interest in the discovery of "silk grass." Although Thomas Harriot identified yucca as a potential for the production of a silklike grosgrain, the greater interest seems to be focused on milkweed (*Asclepias syriaca*). One watercolor of this plant is part of the John White portfolio at the British Museum. It is labeled Wysauke (see fig. 2.10). There is another contemporary watercolor in the British Museum's Sloane manuscripts labeled Wisakon. Milkweed is not mentioned in Harriot's *Briefe and true report*, so it may be one of the two secret commodities to which Harriot alluded. Herbalist John Gerard depicted it as Wisanck in his *Herball* of 1597, where he postulated that the English colonists were still surviving "if neither untimely death by murdering, or pestilence, corrupt aire, bloodie flixes, or some other mortall sicknes hath not destroied them."

Information gathered from the voyages of Samuel Mace and other presently unknown sources appear to have indicated that either English colonists or Native peoples friendly to the English could be found along the coast of Raleigh's Virginia and that a profitable trade for American plant materials could be undertaken. The primary plant material sought by the French-licensed English voyagers on the *Castor and Pollux* and an unnamed consort in 1604–5 was Oyssan or Bissanque. The French cape merchant reported to their Spanish captors that "when the Englishman Guaterrale [Walter Raleigh] came to settle some Englishmen, they took some of the said grass to England and announced that the Indians spun it to make cloth, and they worked it in England and saw that it was silk, like that from China." English interest in the collection of this "silk grass" was to remain strong into the early decades of the 1600s.

Jamestown Searches for the Lost Colony, 1607–9

The Jamestown colonists arrived in Virginia in the spring of 1607. Late that year John Smith was captured by the Pamunkeys and taken to their Indian leader or *weroance*, Opechancanough. Smith recorded that in their conversations, this highly placed and influential member of the Powhatan paramount chiefdom, related information "on certain men at a place called Ocanahonan, clothed like me." Smith was subsequently taken by Pamunkey warriors to meet Powhatan at Werowocomoco on the modern York River (fig. 11.1). There Smith was informed that several days south of Tsenacommacah (the region controlled by Powhatan) were lands of the "Mangoages" (Mangoaks), "Chawwonocks" (Chowanokes), and Roanokes. He was also told of a place called Anone, where the inhabitants "have an abundance of Brasse, and houses walled like ours" (that is, the English at Jamestown).

At some point Smith also heard from Wowinchopunk, a Paspahegh leader, of English people to the south. After New Year's Day 1608, Wowinchopunk was to lead a search party south to unnamed Englishmen. How far they went and what they saw is unclear. A manuscript map called the Smith-Zuniga Map (because Smith created the lost original, but its copy survives in the Spanish archives) that Smith sent to England in June 1608 gives some idea of what they learned or expected to learn (see fig. 10.3). A notation on the map shows a place on the south shore of the James River at or near the modern Pagan River as "here paspahegh and 2 of our men landed to go to panawiock." This panawiock is shown near a watercourse that seems best interpreted as either Cashie River or Salmon Creek in Bertie County. At this locale the map has another notation stating: "here the king of the paspahegh reported our men to be and went to see." Farther to the south was a notation, "here remain the 4 men clothed that came from roonock to okanahowan." The deciphering of what is meant by these notations has consumed the energies of several historians since the map was discovered in a Spanish archive in the later 1800s. Most interpretations have explored the possibilities that they refer to survivors of the Sir Walter Raleigh's colony of 1587 that landed and lived initially on Roanoke Island. John White's account of his voyage of 1590 indicated that the colonists relocated from Roanoke Island. The notations on the Smith-Zuniga Map of 1608 suggest that at least a few of the colonists may have ended up at places named okanhowan, pakerakanick, and panawiock. How many went, when, and why is not indicated.

The search for the lost colonists was deferred when Christopher Newport turned to exploring up the James River and into the Virginia Piedmont in October 1608. After Newport's return to England in December, John Smith talked with Tackonekintaco, a Warraskoyack leader about the possible location of survivors from the Raleigh colonies. A few weeks later, in January 1609, Michael Sicklemore was sent to Chowanoke with two Warraskoyack guides to look for Raleigh's lost colonists and for silk grass. He returned with "little hope and less certainetie of them [that] were left by Sir Walter Rawley." Sicklemore reported the river to be "not great, the people few, the country mostly over growne with pynes, where there did grow here and there straglingly Pemminaw, we call silke grasse. But by the river the ground was good and exceeding furtill." Details on how long Sicklemore was in the Chowan region, where exactly he traveled, and with whom he might have talked were not recorded. There was also no mention of him engaging in any trade activities with the inhabitants of Chowan River region. By the fall of the year, he was reported dead in Nansemond, and no further report of his trip to Chowan is extant.

Soon after, or simultaneous with, the search by Sicklemore in February or March 1609, John Smith sent Nathaniel Powell and Anas Todkill to obtain information on the lost colonists from the Mangoaks. Accurate identification of the Mangoaks is sometimes difficult, but it is likely that this name referred to Iroquoian-speaking groups south of the James River that were outside control of the Powhatan paramount chiefdom (for example, Nottoways, Meherrins, and Tuscaroras). Smith reported discouraging results. He simply wrote: "Nothing we could learn but that they were all dead." This would seem to settle the matter, but a later report published in London suggested that more may have been encountered by Powell and Todkill.

About the same time that these Jamestown colonists were exploring to the south of the James River, two Powhatans, Namontack and Machumps, were visiting London. During the winter of 1609, Machumps talked with William Strachey (who would later come to Virginia and serve as the colony's secretary) about affairs in

Virginia and possible English survivors from the White's Roanoke colony. Reference was made to the survival of several English at a place termed Rittanoe, where four men, two boys, and one "young maid" were believed living under the protection of a leader or wiroane (weroance) named Eyanoco (also written as Gepanacon). The English were said to be "beating" (processing) copper at this town located somewhere south of the James River and likely south of the Roanoke River. Some histories interpret these statements by Machumps to infer that the English at Rittanoe were slaves, hostages, or somehow in bondage to Eyanoco, but there is the plausible inference that Eyanoco was protecting these few people from outside threats. Machumps related that they had fled up the Chowan from "a slaughter at Roanoak" about the time of the arrival of the initial Jamestown colonists in the spring of 1607.

Machumps made reference to two other places in his comments on the fate of the lost colonists: Ocanahonan and Pakerakanick. Of course, it would be very beneficial to know the exact modern sites of these towns, but they have not yet been located with real specificity. About the best that can be said is that Ocanahonan was somewhere on the lower Roanoke River (then called the Moratuc or Moratico River) between modern Roanoke Rapids and the Albemarle Sound, while Pakerakanick was likely somewhere on the modern Tar River between Tarboro and Chocowinity.

By May 1609, the Virginia Company of London envisioned establishing a principal colonial settlement at or near Ocanahonan to access "reputed rich Coppermines at Ritanoe," abundant "silke grasse," and perhaps some contact with the four men "left by Sir Walter Rawley." Later in the year, London saw the publication of the Virginia Company's *True and sincere declaration of the purpose and ends of the plantation begun in Virginia*, which related that two men (likely Powell and Todkill) had discovered within fifty miles of Jamestown some evidence of survivors of the Lost Colony. It was claimed that these two men were denied contact with any of the purported survivors but saw "crosses and letters, the assured testimonies of Christians," cut into trees. Late 1609 also saw the outbreak of what is termed the First Anglo-Powhatan War and an apparent ten-year interruption in English exploration of the Chowan and Roanoke River regions. As Virginia's economy as became grounded on the growth of the cash crop tobacco, interest in a potential copper source near Jamestown appears to have correspondingly diminished.

Occasional and Sporadic Interest and Contact, 1620–40

In March 1620, a committee of the Virginia Company adopted the recommendation of Sir George Yeardley, governor of Virginia, that Marmaduke Rayner be employed to explore the surrounding region in a logical manner "which would produce good benefit to the Plantation." In the summer, Rayner made his exploration "to the Southward to Roanoke." In July 1621, an account of this was read to the officers of the company in London. No copy of the account is known to survive, so it is also unknown whether Rayner entered the Chowan River area.

John Pory, another secretary to the Virginia colony, made a journey in February 1622 to *Chowanoke*. A report of Pory's journey was "preached" by the Reverend Patrick Copland in a London church on April 18. It was said that Pory discovered a "fruitfull Countrie blessed with abundance of Corne, reaped twise a yeere," pine forests, and "a great deale of silk grass." Pory was also reported to have received a piece of copper from the Natives. There was no report that Pory gained any information on the fate of the Roanoke colonists.

The outbreak of the Second Anglo-Powhatan War, in March 1622, again interrupted English involvement in the Chowan River region. Almost a decade and half passed before we hear further

Figure 11.2. Nicholas Comberford, *The south part of Virginia, now the North part of Carolina*, 1657. Royal Museums Greenwich, Charts and Maps, http://collections.rmg.co.uk/collections/objects/540294. © Royal Museums Greenwich.

of an English presence in the area. Surprisingly, new interest focused not on copper, silk grass, and Raleigh's colonists but on the large pine forests already mentioned. And the record of this interest was generated in court records of 1658 in Long Island, New York, regarding a dispute about a swamp.

The records reflect that William Purrier and James Reeve ventured into the Chowan seeking "sperrits resin" (turpentine) in 1636. Somewhere there they met William Salmon, Thomas Reeve, Thomas Terrill, Thomas Benedict, Henry Whitney, and others who had come from the "Summer Isles" (Bermuda). But the venture failed because too many people were involved. It is not certain how far any of them went in seeking to distill pine sap or resin before they redirected their interests to Long Island.

War Comes to the Chowan, 1640–50

Perhaps more frustrating than the absence of historical documentation is when extant historical documentation disagrees with itself. This seems to be the case with notes recorded in an early prayer book from Nansemond County, Virginia. Around 1644, someone wrote in the Basse family prayer book: "Edward Basse sonne of Nath'll & Mary Basse yt unregenerated by the Spirit of God took in marriage one virtuous Indian mayd'n by the Christian name of Mary Tucker and went to live amongst the Shownanocs in Carolina in 1644 A.D. [later entry] He went to Carolina in later years in persute of trade and not in 1644." Did Edward Basse and Mary Tucker Basse move from Nansemond to the Chowan in 1644 as the first note indicates, or did this come later, and the second note is a correction? Where exactly would Edward and Mary have resided in the Chowan region in 1644? Was this move in any way motivated by the outbreak that year of the Third Anglo-Powhatan War?

The English victory—and Powhatan defeat—in that war rearranged the map of Indian nations south of the James River. One result of the war and relocations appears to have been the commencement of what is styled the Anglo-Chowanoke War of 1646. We are uncertain whether the Chowanokes were the identified enemy of the English or the war simply occurred on the Chowan River. The English prevailed in the war and suffered few casualties. In the treaty of October 1646, the Weyanoke tribe ceded all lands east of the Blackwater River up to the James River. The English negotiated this peace agreement with Necotowance, "King of the Indians," but it is unclear whether included any lands of the Chowanokes. It does not seem that Weapemeoc lands were ceded because Nathaniel Batts, George Durant, and others purchased land from Weapemeoc (Yeopim) leaders in the 1650s. Henry Plumpton of Nansemond and Thomas Tuke (Took), veterans of the Anglo-Chowanoke War, are said to have acquired land in 1648 from "Moratuck" (Roanoke River) to "Weyanook" (either Wiccacon Creek or Weyanoke Creek on the west bank of Chowan River). There is no record that Plumpton or Tuke settled anyone on these lands.

Settlement Begins in the 1650s

Interest in English settlement of the Chowan region grew in the early 1650s, and the first permanent settler is recorded by the middle of the decade. In 1650, Edward Bland departed Fort Henry (modern Petersburg) in Virginia for an overland trek south to the area of the Roanoke River. He recounted his exploration in his *Discovery of new Brittaine* (1651). Interpretations of Bland's route do not indicate that he came into the Chowan River area, though he came close when he arrived at the falls of the Roanoke River.

In 1653, the Reverend Roger Green of "Nansemund" acquired a grant of 10,000 acres "on Moratuck or Roanoake river . . . south side of Choan river and branches thereof." The bounds of this grant are not known today. Whether it referred to lands on the west side of the Chowan River or the south side of modern Albemarle Sound and Roanoke River is somewhat unclear. There is no record that Green settled on his granted lands. In 1656, Green was in Virginia, probably at Jamestown instead of Nansemond, advocating for more towns in Virginia.

In 1654 or 1655, carpenter Robert Bodnam built a house–trading post for Nathaniel Batts at the confluence of the Chowan and Roanoke Rivers. A pictogram on a map from 1657 shows the location of this house. Just to the north, there was drawn a creek labeled Flett's Creek, no doubt a misreading by a copyist of "Batts Creek" (fig. 11.2).

Early settlers after 1657 were largely Quakers who settled on the Perquimans and Pasquotank Rivers on the north shore of Albemarle Sound. Some people also settled on the south shore,

Figure 11.3. James Lancaster, *Albemarle Sound, North Carolina*, Blathwayte Atlas, London, 1679. John Carter Brown Library, Map Collection 8189. Courtesy John Carter Brown Library.

as shown in the 1670s on a map in the Blathwayt Atlas. It shows houses there but none up the Chowan River beyond Salmon Creek (fig. 11.3). By this time, Indian leaders had already responded to settlers' desire for land north of the Albemarle Sound. Two rare surviving property transactions record mid-seventeenth-century colonial purchases of lands from Weapemeoc (Yeopim) weroance Kiscutanaweh or Kilcocanen (Kiscotanan?). Again, there were unspecific references to other settlers. Both of those land purchases were for tracts well to the east of the Chowan River and may indicate population contraction and group relocation of the Weapemeocs. There may also be some evidence of their growing cultural assimilation with the English in Lower Norfolk County.

To sum up, there is no evidence of English settlement and occupation along the Chowan River between the time of the secondhand reports to Jamestown of 1607–8 and the Batts trading post record of 1655. There are hints of interest in the area and some efforts toward securing land grants in the area of the lower Chowan, but there is no evidence of contact longer than brief explorations, surveys, and military incursions. There is likewise no documentation of English traders becoming established in the region before the arrival of Nathaniel Batts in the 1650s. This does not preclude the possibility of European goods reaching the Chowan region through undocumented activities, but it would seemingly limit such goods to those types identified through historical and archaeological research of the Anglo-Indian trade of the period. And archaeological research informs us that English pottery was neither traded to Indians nor wanted by them.

POSTSCRIPT

First Colony Foundation continues to make new discoveries beyond Site X on the banks of the Chowan River. Surveys of fields and woodland north of Site X led to excavations in 2019–21 of Site Y, at a waterside bluff on land belonging to Bertie County. There, our team gathered data from ground-penetrating radar and guided the enthusiastic and increasingly skillful volunteer excavators, who screened soil excavated from seventy-two five-foot-by-five-foot test squares. They unearthed ceramic sherds from the Roanoke Colony period, which were carefully examined by Beverly "Bly" Straube, Jamestown Settlement senior curator and First Colony Foundation curator, and Jamestown Rediscovery curator Merry A. Outlaw. These two experts on early colonial material culture identified a wider variety of sixteenth-century European ceramics than at Site X: Surrey-Hampshire Border ware, North Devon baluster jars, London redware, and Essex fine redware, along with Spanish olive jars, Frechen stoneware from Germany, and Martincamp stoneware from France. The sherds represent food and drink preparation, consumption, and storage, indicating that Roanoke Colony settlers resided at the site. Interpretations of the evidence suggest occupation perhaps by a dozen individuals of a single extended family with unrelated servants or by several smaller family units.

We are confident that these Roanoke Colony Period ceramics cannot date to the time of permanent English settlement initiated by Nathaniel Batts in 1655 some two miles south of Site Y. A comparison of key ceramics from Site Y with their occurrence on more than twenty pre-1650 sites in Virginia, as well as the absence of colonial tobacco pipe stems with large bore holes, provides evidence that there was no undocumented seventeenth-century English presence there. Similarly, the lack of Late Woodland Native material reinforces earlier conclusions that the artifacts unearthed at Site X do not represent European goods traded to the Native American population.

Site Y is the second discovery of Elizabethan artifacts in FCF's target area in Bertie County. Just as eighth-grade science class taught us that observations must be repeated to be valid, so an Elizabethan presence in Bertie County is now validated. Site Y has substantiated the theory, based on Site X, that the patch on the British Museum's map *La Virginea Pars* indicates an unsuspected goal in Sir Walter Raleigh's plans. This finding was not entirely unsuspected: North Carolina historians Samuel A. Ashe and Thomas C. Parramore had both advocated seeking evidence of the Lost

Colony in the vicinity, as has James Horn in this volume.

Site Y further substantiates our conclusion that Site X was a short-lived habitation of a small group of the colonists who left Roanoke Island after the return to England of Governor John White in the late summer of 1587. The ultimate fates of the individual settlers remain unresolved, but these discoveries speak to the actions that the colonists took following their departure from Roanoke Island. Most prominent historians of the Roanoke ventures no longer believe in a single large relocation site but instead surmise that the colonists dispersed into numerous small settlement groups, just as Raleigh's first Roanoke colony dispersed due to a food shortage in 1586.

Site Y excavations have created a more nuanced picture of Elizabethans on the Chowan River. Site X suggested a family of refugees protected by the warriors of an adjacent village. Site Y has no such native settlement nor any evidence of their presence. We must conclude that the Chowanoke king Menatonon, Governor Ralph Lane's ally, permitted Raleigh's colonists to settle on designated lands where they could provide for themselves. If so, other farming families would have also been given sites for planting and probably surrounding areas for hunting and fishing. The vision now is one of contact and cooperation, not the old story of conflict and failure on Roanoke Island. The families from 1587 settled where they intended, fifty miles inland. They lived not in the "Cittie of Ralegh"—a city of dreams—but among the Chowanoke people in scattered settlements on the "goodly high land" that Ralph Lane had seen on the Chowan's west bank.

We conclude from a decade of research that a number of Sir Walter Raleigh's settlers of 1587 acted on their intentions of moving fifty miles into the mainland and that Site X and Y are two locations where some of these colonists were present and active. But Site Y does not solve the Lost Colony mystery. It answers the old question, "Where did the settlers go?" But the new question is, "What happened to them there?" Their stay appears to have been brief. What happened to change their situation? Disease, famine, or enemies?

The recent archaeology at Site Y combined with the earlier finds at Site X provides strong encouragement for continued research in the project area as funding becomes available to support additional fieldwork and postexcavation analysis. How many colonists were present at Sites X and Y, what interactions occurred between the Algonquians and their new English neighbors, and what parts of the archaeological record might be found elsewhere? The goal of our announced "Project 1587" is to discover Elizabethan America, 1587–1607. We have immediate plans for underwater archaeological survey and testing in Salmon Creek itself. Beyond that, archaeological survey and testing for areas south of the creek are being considered. And beyond that fieldwork, there remain the other towns of the Chowanoke kingdom and, between them, the likely sites for Elizabethan farmsteads.

Dr. William Kelso, emeritus director of archaeology at Jamestown Rediscovery, eloquently said, "What has been found so far at Site Y in Bertie County appears to me to solve one of the greatest mysteries in Early American history, the odyssey of the 'Lost Colony.' And now, like Jamestown, knowing more about where the history of the English-American nation began is a crucial step toward a full understanding of what the American nation has become."

Further Readings

Artifacts

Egan, Geoff. *Lead Cloth Seals and Related Items in the British Museum*. British Museum Occasional Paper 93. London: British Museum, 1994.

Noël Hume, Ivor. *A Guide to Artifacts of Colonial America*. 2nd ed. Philadelphia: University of Pennsylvania Press, 2001.

Straube, Beverly. "'A Sure Token of Their Being There': Artefacts from England's Colonial Ventures at Roanoke and Jamestown." In *Exploring Atlantic Transitions: Archaeologies of Transience and Permanence in New Found Lands*, edited by Peter E. Pope, 190–201. Woodbridge, UK: Boydell Press, 2013.

Cartography

Barber, Peter. "England I: Pageantry, Defense and Government: Maps at Court to 1550; England II: Monarchs, Maps and Ministers, 1550–1625." In *Monarchs, Ministers, and Maps: The Emergence of Cartography as a Tool of Government in Early Modern Europe*, edited by David Buisseret, 26–98. Chicago: University of Chicago Press, 1992.

Barber, Peter, and Tom Harper. *Magnificent Maps*. London: British Library, 2010.

Harvey, P. D. A. *The Hereford World Map: Medieval World Maps and Their Context*. London: British Library, 2006.

———. *Maps in Tudor England*. London: British Library, 1993.

———. *Medieval Maps*. London: British Library, 1991.

Wallis, Helen, ed. *Raleigh and Roanoke: The British Library Exhibit Hosted by the North Carolina Museum of History*. Raleigh: America's Four Hundredth Anniversary Committee and North Carolina Department of Cultural Resources, 1985.

Woodward, David, ed. *The History of Cartography*. Vol. 3: *Cartography in the European Renaissance*. Chicago: University of Chicago Press, 2007.

Jamestown

Barbour, Philip L., ed. *The Complete Works of Captain John Smith*. 3 vols. Chapel Hill: University of North Carolina Press, 1986.

Horn, James. *A Land as God Made It: Jamestown and the Birth of America*. New York: Basic Books, 2005.

Kupperman, Karen Ordahl. *Indians and English: Facing Off in Early America*. Ithaca, NY: Cornell University Press, 2000.

Rountree, Helen C. *The Powhatans Indians of Virginia: Their Traditional Culture*. Norman: University of Oklahoma Press, 1989.

Strachey, William. *The Historie of Travell in Virginia Britania* (1612). Edited by Louis B. Wright and Virginia Freud. London: Hakluyt Society, 1953.

John White

Ambers, Janet, Joanna Russell, David Saunders, and Kim Sloan. "'Hidden History?' Examination of Two Patches on John White's Map of 'Virginia.'" *British Museum Technical Research Bulletin* 6 (2012): 47–54.

Sloan, Kim. *A New World: England's First View of America*. Chapel Hill: University of North Carolina Press, and London: British Museum Publications, 2006. See also Collections Online on the British Museum website: registration numbers 1906,0509.1.1 to 76.

———, ed. *European Visions: American Voices*. British Museum Research Publication 172. London: British Museum, 2009. https://webarchive.nationalarchives.

gov.uk/ukgwa/20190801111839/https://www.britishmuseum.org/research/publications/research_publications_series/2009/european_visions.aspx.

Roanoke

Cumming, William P. *The Southeast in Early Maps*. 3rd ed. Chapel Hill: University of North Carolina Press, 1998.

Harriot, Thomas. *Briefe and True Report*. Frankfurt: Theodor de Bry, 1590.

Horn, James. *A Kingdom Strange: The Brief and Tragic History of the Lost Colony of Roanoke*. New York: Basic Books, 2010.

Klingelhofer, Eric. "Tudor Overseas Fortifications: A Review and Typology." In *First Forts: Essays on the Archaeology of Proto-Colonial Fortifications*, 65–83. Leiden, NL: Brill Academic Press, 2010.

Kupperman, Karen Ordahl. *Roanoke: The Abandoned Colony*. 2nd ed. Lanham, MD: Rowman and Littlefield, 2007.

Oberg, Michael Leroy. *The Head in Edward Nugent's Hand: Roanoke's Forgotten Indians*. Philadelphia: University of Pennsylvania Press, 2008.

Parramore, Thomas C. "The 'Lost Colony' Found: A Documentary Perspective." *North Carolina Historical Review* 78, no. 1 (2001): 67–83.

Powell, William S. "Who Were the Roanoke Colonists?" In *Raleigh and Quinn: The Explorer and His Boswell*, edited by H. G. Jones, 51–67. Chapel Hill: North Caroliniana Society, 1987.

Quinn, David Beers. *The Roanoke Voyages, 1584–1590*. London: Hakluyt Society, 1955; repr. New York: Dover, 1991.

———. *Set Fair for Roanoke: Voyages and Colonies, 1484–1606*. Chapel Hill: University of North Carolina Press, 1985.

Rountree, Helen C. *Manteo's World: Native American Life in Carolina's Sound Country before and after the Lost Colony*. Chapel Hill: University of North Carolina Press, 2021.

Simard, Suzanne. *Finding the Mother Tree: Discovering the Wisdom of the Forest*. New York: Alfred A. Knopf, 2021.

Thrush, Coll. *Indigenous London: Native Travelers at the Heart of Empire*. New Haven, CT: Yale University Press, 2016. Chapter 2 discusses the Syllabary's design, with an image of the surviving page.

Ward, Trawick H., and R. P. Stephen Davis Jr. *Time before History: The Archaeology of North Carolina*. Chapel Hill: University of North Carolina Press, 1998.

Contributors

Mr. Peter Barber served as head of Map Collections at the British Library from 2001 to 2015, directing the project to recatalog and digitize King George III's Topographical Collection. In addition to scholarly works on medieval world maps and the role of cartography by early modern European governments, he has authored and edited several popular books on the history of maps.

Mr. Phillip W. Evans is a seventeen-year veteran of the National Park Service, having served as historian at Fort Raleigh for most of that time, becoming one of the leading historians of the Roanoke Colony. Currently an attorney, he is a member of the North Caroliniana Society and is president of First Colony Foundation.

Dr. James Horn is president of the Jamestown Rediscovery Foundation, affiliated with Preservation Virginia. Previously, he was vice president of research and historical interpretation at the Colonial Williamsburg Foundation. The author of numerous books on early colonial history, he is a historian on the First Colony Foundation Board of Directors.

Dr. Eric Klingelhofer is emeritus professor of history at Mercer University and vice president of research for First Colony Foundation. An expert in medieval archaeology and protocolonial archaeology, he specializes in the study of early English colonization in Ireland, the Caribbean, and North America.

Dr. Karen Ordahl Kupperman is emerita professor of history at New York University, where she created the program in Atlantic history. She is one of the leading historians of early English colonization in the New World, with a further specialization in Anglo-Native relations.

Mr. Nicholas M. Luccketti specializes in early colonial archaeology in the Chesapeake area. Formerly lead archaeologist at both Colonial Williamsburg and Jamestown Rediscovery, he is president of the James River Institute for Archaeology and a vice president of research with First Colony Foundation.

Dr. Kim Sloan is curator emerita of pre-1880 British Drawings and Watercolors at the British Museum. Following the exhibit in 2007 of John White's drawings and their definite publication in *A New World: England's First View of America*, she coordinated the scientific analysis of the map *La Virginea Pars* that revealed hidden images of the Roanoke colony's explorations.

Dr. Beverly "Bly" Straube is the acknowledged expert on early English colonial artifacts. She served as curator and collections manager at Jamestown Rediscovery for nearly twenty years and has since joined the staff of the Jamestown-Yorktown Foundation. She is the curator on record for First Colony Foundation.

Mr. Edward Clay Swindell is the regional archaeologist for the US Naval Facilities Engineering Command Mid-Atlantic region. A recognized expert on the subject of Carolina Algonquian archaeology, he serves on the First Colony Foundation Board of Directors.

Index

Italic page numbers refer to illustrations.